Zombie Apocalypse

How To Survival Prepping And Zombie Defense

(A Guide For Surviving A Zombie Apocalypse With Homemade Survival Kit)

Michael Emery

Published By **John Kembrey**

Michael Emery

Zombie Apocalypse: How To Survival Prepping And Zombie Defense (A Guide For Surviving A Zombie Apocalypse With Homemade Survival Kit)

ISBN 978-1-77485-697-0

Legal & Disclaimer

The information contained in this ebook is not designed to replace or take the place of any form of medicine or professional medical advice. The information in this ebook has been provided for educational & entertainment purposes only.

The information contained in this book has been compiled from sources deemed reliable, and it is accurate to the best of the Author's knowledge; however, the Author cannot guarantee its accuracy and validity and cannot be held liable for any errors or omissions. Changes are periodically made to this book. You must consult your doctor or get professional medical advice before using any of the suggested remedies, techniques, or information in this book.

TABLE OF CONTENTS

Introduction

It could be a viral outbreak. It could be a bio-chemical terrorist attack. It could also be a heaven-sent retaliation. It could even be a curse from a generation past, sent to make us pay for a long-overdue debt.

It's no longer a question if it's going to happen. It's more of a question of are you ready for it?

Unlike a nuclear apocalypse or collapse of a global market, the stakes are different when it comes to a zombie apocalypse. From preparation to everyday tactics, major changes should be made to ensure you outlast an outbreak.

This manual is designed to help you prepare and survive a zombie apocalypse. From telling you what to prepare to what to do, you'll know almost everything you need to make sure that you come out on top of such a catastrophe.

Besides provisions, materials and equipment, you will also read about survival mechanics during encounters to ensure that you walk away with your humanity in any given situation. In a world where everyone is trying to turn you into one of them, your sanity and

humanity are your most prized possession. Here, you will learn techniques to safeguard those very possessions.
With proper preparation and training, you can become a stronghold for your family and loved ones when the time comes that humanity faces their last stand against their own former flesh.

Chapter 1: It Has Now Hit the Fan

Had fun with all the zombie jokes, did you? Well, the undead . . . stuff . . . has now hit the proverbial fan one way or the other and you've decided to get with the program. Welcome to the new reality. Don't worry, if you're not planning on getting tough, it'll be a short ride. Bloody, but short.

Cultivate an Attitude of Survival

To paraphrase a cool little wrinkled dude with a light saber, “Live or live not. There is no try.” If you don’t have an attitude of survival already, get yourself in the game -- now.

I’ll always try to talk to both the before and the after crowd.

If you're reading this in advance of the coming apocalypse, I have good news -- you'll probably make it once the world heads south. Preparation is everything. You still have time. Not much. But some.

If you're hunkered down in some trashed bookstore peering at the page with a flashlight, turn that damn thing off, stuff this book in your backpack, and get the hell out of there!

Stopping to read in an unsecured location in the middle of an apocalypse is not a great idea. It's a wonder you've lived this long. I'll help you, but first, get some place safe — and be quiet doing it!

First Things First. They're Not Human!

If you're one of those bleeding heart types, you need to get over that sentimental streak pretty damn fast unless you want to bleed for real — and then spend the rest of your undead life shambling around with your new zombie scout den buddies.

I don't care if that zombie standing in front of you does look like your grandma. Heck, I don't care if she IS your Grandma -- she is not human. Don't try to talk to her. Don't try to feed her. Don't try to domesticate her. Put. Her. Down.

Two reasons. One, you'll live another day and two, even if she isn’t human now, she was once. Have a little respect. When you kill a zombie, you're putting a former human out of his or her misery. Consider it your good deed for the day and hope to the high heavens someone will do the same for you if it ever comes to that.

Why Are You Still Alive?

That's a really good question, and I don't mean, "what are you doing right to not get ripped to shreds." I mean, "why are you bothering to stay alive?"

People who make it have goals. What are you hanging around for? What's your long-term strategy?

Again, if the apocalypse hasn't happened, congrats. You're putting some thought into why you're taking up space on the planet. That's more than most people do.

I gotta tell you, on any given day I look at a lot of my fellow humans and think, "Wow, that's oxygen we're never gonna get back in the atmosphere."

Let's consider your raison d'etre, buddy. That's French for, "Why am I fricking bothering?"

You want to cure the zombies and save the world.

Dude. Please.

If your previous job was the head of the CDC, then go for it. Hell, if that's the case, you're hold up in Atlanta with enough food, water, and power to watch all the rest of us get chomped up for kibbles and bits. Knock yourself out.
If you were flipping fries at Mickey D's? You've been reading too many comic books. Oh, excuse me. "Graphic novels." Whatever. You need a new goal. Now.

You're trying to get back to your family.

I'm not giving you grief about that one, brother. Having somebody else to live for is a big reason to stay in the game. Don't let anybody tell you otherwise. If you think your wife or your husband or your kids are still out there, then move freaking heaven and earth to find them.

You want to build a safe haven for yourself.

Okay, you can go all lone wolf Unibomber after the apocalypse and I get that. I'm guessing you've already seen people looting stores and running each other down in the streets. If you have any sense, you headed the other direction fast.

One of the first things you absolutely have to do when this all breaks is get away from people, but then, when things calm down a little? Find yourself some people.

You can't go it all by yourself forever. First off, you have to sleep sometimes. Second, you'll go bonkers after awhile if all you do every day is kill people who just don't get it that they're already dead.

Remember that movie with Tom Hanks on the island where he talked to the volleyball for two hours? At the very least, get yourself a volleyball. Yeah, some of us are introverts and spend more time alone than other people, but under normal circumstances a trip to 7-Eleven at least reminds you that you're not the last living person on the planet.

You want to find a new way to live.

That one right there will work for you. Old normal is gone, new normal is here. Make it work.

Real survivors are flexible. Man, you better have Plans A through G already figured out and turn on a dime when you need Plan H.

Do NOT get locked into one way of doing anything.

Keep your cool no matter what hits the fan. You can fall apart later. In the moment, keep your head and keep thinking.

That right, I'm saying it again and I'll keep saying it. The ability to think is the greatest tool at your disposal. You can. They can't.

Be curious. Be creative. Look at everything around you with new eyes. Everything's a potential tool. It doesn't matter what it used to do for you, what can it do NOW? You know that idea of re-purposing old stuff? You're basically in a position to re-purpose the whole world.

And totally keep your sense of humor. You know the Gun Owner's Prayer? The last line reads, "Let NOT my last thought be, if I only had a gun, and Lord if today is truly the day that you call me home, let me die in a pile of empty brass."

Me? I think it should read, "Let me die laughing in a pile of empty brass." You can't take this stuff too seriously. Come on, admit it, you watched The Walking Dead. Best line ever? Herschel after the fall of the farm in season two.

"Christ promised the resurrection of the dead. I just thought he had something different in mind."

This stuff is just freaking priceless.

Why is This Happening to Me?

Oh for God's sake. Do we really need to waste time on the "why me" bullshit?

Fine. Chances are good nobody really knows why the apocalypse is upon us. There are some major things to think about though if you just insist on trying to figure it out -- especially if you're one of those, "there has to be a way to put it all back like it was" types.

Back in August 2010, Sarah Boseley, the health editor for The Guardian wrote an article called "Are You Ready for a World Without Antibiotics?" and pretty much nailed it in my opinion:

"The era of antibiotics is coming to a close. In just a couple of generations, what once appeared to be miracle medicines have been beaten into ineffectiveness by the bacteria they were designed to knock out. Once, scientists hailed the end of infectious diseases. Now, the post-antibiotic apocalypse is within sight."

How many times didn't you finish that prescription because you were feeling better? Well hang your head in shame now. You helped engineer the super bugs and one of them went all zombie on our collective butts.

All it took was just one sick person getting on an airplane and forget about quarantining squat. If you still have time, go pick up a cheerful little tome by Matthew Stein called When Disaster Strikes:

". . . with bacteria developing antibiotic resistance faster than we can develop new medicines, and viruses' ability to 'gene swap' genetic material between deadly diseases with low infection rates . . . highly infectious diseases . . . it is only a matter of time before the roulette wheel of natural genetic selection and mutation deals humanity a crippling blow."

Yeah, baby. What happens in Vegas stays in Vegas . . . until the roulette balls jumps out of the wheel. So, I think that's what happened. Mutant resurrection flu virus from hell. Now, can we get practical again?

Where Are You Now?

If you're still bummed, and okay, granted, this does kinda suck, work on the "why you are" and "why did this happen" and get that all figured out for yourself. Trust me, you'll have more than enough time to contemplate the meaning of life – assuming you manage to actually stay alive.

For right now, let's talk about the where you are. Sitting in your recliner knocking back a cold Sam Adams on a perfectly normal day? Cool. You're golden for now.

Apocalypse in progress? If you're in a city, take what you need and bug the hell out. Get into the countryside as fast as you can. You'll up your lifespan the minute you cross the city limits.

Don't make the mistake of trying to get supplies at a mall or a trashed grocery store -- at least not during the initial panic. Those places will be great to scavenge in the future when the bulk of your fellow humans have turned into Zeta Zeta Zeta sorority pledges.

(Get it? Zeta. Zombie. The "z" thing. Oh come on. I said you can't take this shit too seriously. Lighten up. You're not dead yet . . . I hope.)

In the opening days, even weeks of the apocalypse, people will flock to stores and fight like rabid dogs for the last package of ramen. Stay. Away.

If you have to try to get into a store, think Mom and Pop joints on the edge of town, and scope the place out carefully. Civilization frays really fast when people are scared out of their minds. Living humans are just as dangerous to you as dead ones during those first waves of sheer panic. They’re not thinking about anybody but themselves.

If the apocalypse is impending, start making plans for where will you go when it hits. As you're reading this book and learning about strategy, fortifications, and storing supplies, figure out where you can stockpile your stuff and how you'll get there when the time comes.

Right now, let's just start small.

Chapter 2: Buy an Altoids ® Tin

Zombies hate bad breath.

Sorry. Took the low hanging fruit on that one. Back to our regularly scheduled apocalypse.

An Altoids ® tin is big enough to hold adequate minimal survival gear to get you through a few days if you're stuck away from home and your main source of supplies.

In survivalist speak, we're talking about an "every day carry" kit – something small enough to have on your person at all times so you can respond effectively to "high probability events" like the zombie apocalypse.

Ideally, you will have a cache of supplies at both your home and a remote location, but let's start with what you can carry on your person every day.

Emergency Supplies as "Every Day Carry"

Pretty much everybody uses some kind of gear bag these days to lug around all the crap we think we need to get us through the day. Not using the bag we're already carrying to keep an EDC kit with you so you're ready to bug out at a minute's notice is kinda stupid. I'm just saying.

Now, a word of caution. Be sure not to run your mini survival gear through security at the airport, though. The TSA gets all upset about things like razor blades and pocket knives. They're narrow minded that way.
Before the power goes out, you can get on YouTube and find about a jillion examples of Altoids ® tin rigs. It's almost a hobby among survivalists to create the perfect miniature survival kit.

And actually, treating your EDC like a hobby while you have time to tinker and refine the contents is an excellent plan. I'm going to run down some ideas about things that you can include, but there are no absolutes here. Your environment should affect all your preparation decisions. Urban survival is very different from wilderness survival.

Obviously you're limited by the size of the tin, but that's the point. Design something you can have with you at all times.

The Tin Itself

Start with a standard size Altoids ® tin, which will set you back about $1.50. Here's how much room you'll be working with:

th inches (9.68 cm)

th inches (6.19 cm)

Secure the tin when it's closed with a couple of thick rubber bands or ranger bands (more on those in a second.) Sure, using the bands will keep the lid in place, but they're also just one more useful piece of equipment crammed into the overall package. As long as you maintain the low profile of the tin, which is the whole point of this exercise, affix whatever you want to the outside with tape.
Think Outside the Tin

Ranger bands are a good alternate to plain old rubber bands and they're certainly something you want around in your larger cache of supplies. They're basically made out of bicycle inner tube and are super tough and strong.

The potential uses are limited by your imagination and needs only. Sure, you can lash stuff with your available cordage -- or use a couple of crossed ranger bands and get better tension and strength than you'll ever manage cross wrapping cord or wire.

Tops you'll spend $10-$15.

If you're not intending to open the tin often, seal the lid with a piece of black electrical tape to make it more waterproof. It'll stay sticky forever. Or go for Gorilla Tape. That stuff would survive any apocalypse.

I actually prefer putting the tin in a small, heavy duty Ziplock ® type bag and then securing the rubber bands in place over that.

My philosophy is to include every potentially useful and re-usable component possible. Weight isn't a factor, plus, by the time you're done the tin will be so crammed full of supplies it won't rattle.

If it does, you can always put in a couple of extra cotton balls, which, as you will see, do double duty for first aid and as tinder to start a fire.
Understand that the tin itself is part of your usable survival gear. You can purify water by boiling it in the tin, and you can even use the tin as a small "stove" for heating food. The material is durable enough to withstand a low flame.

Face it, when the apocalypse hits, you will have missed lunch that day because you're just that lucky. As I've already pointed out, scavenging in grocery stores in the beginning will not be a good idea. Do yourself a favor and start carrying 2 or 3 packets of instant oatmeal around in your regular day bag.

If you're on the run and just trying to stay alive at the moment, you don't want to be weighted down with extra junk. You have to eat, but you also have to stay mobile. I guess you could beat a zombie to death with a can of Campbell's Chunky Soup, but I don't plan to test the theory any time soon.

At this stage of the game, a few spoonfuls of hot oatmeal will keep you alive, and you can easily shove them in your pocket if you have to ditch your larger bag to be more mobile.

(Don't throw the envelopes away! They're designed to hold water for mixing the oatmeal, and paper is always potential tinder.)

Remember, the apocalypse won't have you starved down yet. Two-thirds of all Americans are overweight. For the first month or so, you'll probably have plenty of fat to burn. Think of the whole thing as kind of a zombie zumba diet.
So yeah, Altoids ® tin oatmeal may taste like day old brick mortar, but all you need to make it is a little water.

Inside the Lid

Use the space inside the lid of the Altoids ® tin to tape small flat items like a:

UCO makes a Stormproof Match Kit with 25 matches and 3 strikers for $6.75. Use one of the strikers for your Altoids ® kit and include 2 or 3 of the matches.

You can also tape down elements of a fishing kit in the lid, but the practicality of that will vary by circumstance.

Mini Fishing Kit

You probably won't be hanging out in the bass boat after the world goes to hell, but here's what you'll need to if you do decide to include the fishing kit option. Almost any insect will work for bait.

to put in a branch for threading your line.

-
-

Tape the flat stuff in the top of the box (or to the sides of the base.) Use a section of hollow plastic pen to hold the sinkers, with your line wrapped tight around it. Seal the ends of the tube off with squares of duct tape.

Emergency Signaling Options

Another option is to take a flat piece of mirror and affix it to the inside of the lid. One of the best places to find a mirror that works is to get one of those travel folding hairbrushes with a mirror in the handle. Just pop the piece out and it will be the right length for the tin's lid.

A mirror is useful in a variety of ways, including emergency signaling. If you need to send a silent distress signal the flash of light from a mirror is clearly visible at a distance.

Of course, if you're a hardcore survivalist, you'll know how to use an emergency mirror to send messages in Morse code, but unless you're part of a group, the chances that anyone who can read the code are pretty thin.

If you buy an actual survival mirror, the unit will have a built in aiming hole so you can tell where the flash of light will hit when you signal. That's a nice option if you plan on using the light to distract zombies and head them off in another direction.

We'll talk more about what zombies can and can't do physically and mentally in another chapter, but basically, you can get their attention with sound and motion and use it to their advantage when you need them to be someplace other than trying to knock down the door of the house you're hiding in.

Ultimate Survival Technologies sells a cool little Starflash Signal Mirror for $5.85 that measures 2" x 3". It's unbreakable, will float if you drop it, and is 90% more reflective than glass.

Think Outside the Tin

Staying quiet and staying invisible is to your advantage in the apocalypse. Remember, everything is a tool and everything has multiple uses.

Having a mirror will also help you get a view around a corner without sticking your head out and giving yourself away. You can also use your cordage to lash the mirror to a stick and extend your reach if you need to look over a wall or similar obstacle to reconnoiter an area.

(Man. I love writing this survival stuff. Where else can you use a word like reconnoiter and not sound like a total tool?)

Another signaling option is an aluminum emergency camping whistle. I've seen these packaged in sets of three for around $8. They're loud enough to be heard at considerable distances, but remember zombies come to sounds so only use your whistle if:

(1) you want the undead headed in a particular direction.
(2) you're up to your shorts in re-animated rotting corpses and you're trying to get someone to help you.

I'd fold up about a 2' x 2' square of heavy duty aluminum foil and tape it to the bottom of the tin. It's reflective enough to be used for signaling, or you can use it to line the tin for cooking — or for that matter, fashion the stuff into a crude bowl.

Fire Starting and Cordage

Some variation of the above is about all you're going to get in the lid of your tin. In the bottom of the box, I'd say you're definitely going to want a Bic-type lighter for fire starting (four for about $6) in addition to your waterproof matches.

Wrap about 20 feet of strong hemp cord around the lighter just to make good use of the space. Never miss out on a chance to combine items in this fashion.

While we're on the subject of cordage, include about 10 yards of dental floss in your kit. Just bust a box of it open and put the whole roll in the tin. That stuff is tough, and you can use it to sew things together -- yourself included, which is why you taped that sewing needle in the lid.

First Aid Supplies

In addition to the dental floss and needle for stitching up wounds, take a length of a plain drinking straw, fill it with Neosporin, pinch the

ends, and melt them closed with your lighter, then wrap the dental floss around the tube.
If you don't have the guts to take a needle to yourself, you might be a little too squeamish for the apocalypse period, but a small tube of Crazy Glue is also an option.

Yeah, it's probably toxic as all git out, but that's the least of your worries when corpses are getting up and wandering around.

Use a small Ziplock ® bag, like the kind jewelry comes in to hold one or two doses each of ibuprofen and Benadryl ®.

Keep this package flat and small. Clearly the ibuprofen is for pain, but if you do manage to get yourself in a really secure location and you can't sleep, the Benadryl ® will calm you down enough to get some rest.

Think Outside the Tin

Clearly if you need specific medication or if you're a diabetic, you have to think about your special needs. Ditch the fishing kit and make room for the required pills. You can also use sealed straws to hold sugar.

If you're allergic to insect bites, find the smallest Epipen ® you can get your hands on. If it won't fit in the tin, make sure it's still with you every day. You'll be doing a lot of hiding in the opening days of the apocalypse, probably in dark places where critters have already made their home.

Be a hell of a note to survive the apocalypse and get taken out by a spider.

Include a sturdy pair of tweezers, a couple of adhesive bandages (also known as Band-Aids), one or two alcohol prep pads (which can also be used for starting a fire since alcohol is flammable), and a small gauze pad.

Cotton balls are also an option. They're good for first aid uses and as tinder. Also, when they're stuffed in the kit, they'll keep it from rattling. Remember, when in Zombieland, silence is golden.

Light Source

Definitely get a light source in there. The Streamlight 73001 Nano Light is an excellent choice for under $10. It's made of machined aluminum and it outfitted with a 5mm white LED. The whole thing is only 1.47 inches long and you'll get about 8 hours of declining usable output.

Find some red transparent cellophane and cut a square large enough to be folded over the end of the Streamlight and secured in place with one of your rubber bands. Red light preserves night vision but provides enough illumination to work by.

The snap hook on the end of the light is a multi-purpose bonus. You can either remove the clip and use it as a secure attachment for another purpose, or tie on some cord and suspend the light to create a small work lamp.

Some people opt for those little keychain LEDs you pinch together with your fingers. They're definitely flatter and will fit better in a crowded tin. Here's a tip. If you go that route, take your knife and work the battery and the LED out of the plastic container. All you have to do to get the LED to burn is just clip it on the battery.

Lay out a piece of electrical tape and put the battery and the LED on it, then cover them with a second piece of tape. That's about as flat and compact a flashlight as you could ask for and you can re-purpose the tape.

Cutting Tool

Lots of home-brewed, armchair, "I kill zombies in video games" types well tell you to go get a cheap knife down at Wal-Mart, break out the blade, and put that in your mini kit. Yeah. Right. Cause I'm looking to do the end of the world on a budget and lose several fingers in the process.

Do not go the cheap route when it comes to your cutting tool. Buy the CRKT RKS MK5 for about $20-$25. The high quality 3.81-inch blade sits in a fixed handle. Total weight: 1 ounce with the included sheath. The whole package is small enough to fit angled across the base of the tin.

You won't get enough reach with a knife like this to put a zombie down, but thanks to the open handle and the holes at the top of the blade, you can lash the MK5 to a long, thick pole. Until you can get to your own supplies or acquire a better weapon, this rig should get you out of solitary zombie encounters.

As for a herd? Run Forest, run.

Think Outside the Tin

One thing you have to consider in putting a kit like this together are your specific survival needs. I absolutely think you have to have a knife in your kit, but you might also want a cut down hacksaw blade.

If you're in an urban survival situation, it's possible cutting through a padlock will be on your anti-bucket list. Some of the stray bits of tape in the kit folded over the ends of the blade can create serviceable saw "handles."

Sure, it'll take for fricking ever to get through the hasp, but if the prize on the other side is your now undead buddy's prized Harley so you can get you the hell out of Dodge, go for it!

One of those flexible hand chainsaws is also an option, but they're too big to fit in your tin and they weigh 5-6 ounces. The SaberCut Survival Saw by Ultimate Survival Technologies ($30) is pretty much the cream of the crop in this genre of survival cutting tools should you decide to pick one up.

Other Useful Items

Don't count on navigating by landmarks alone. Find yourself a little mini compass to the tune of $5 or so. These little babies are often called "button" compasses. They're not the most accurate things out there, but they'll do in a pinch and they're literally no larger than a coat button. If you have a map or can score one, all the better.

A simple folded up coffee filter will filter big debris out of water, but I'd definitely get some water purification tablets. A package of 10 Ef Chlor tablets will get you a long way. That's enough to clean up more than 50 gallons of water for $10 and they pack is flat enough to fit in the tin. (I'll talk more about water contamination here in a bit.)

A two-pack of Military P-51 can openers will only set you back about $2.50 and will do a better job of opening a can than your knife. Truth be told, though, you don't need a can opener at all.

Find a flat, rough surface -- just plain old concrete -- and rub the top of a can back and forth until you've scraped the edges down. Just squeeze the can and the lid pops right off. (I'd recommend practicing a few times, but once you get the hang of it this trick works great.)

Summary

As crazy as it sounds, one of the reasons I hear all the time for not preparing for a disaster of any kind is how much all the supplies will cost.
Are you freaking kidding me? Nobody ever saved their life in the middle of a crisis and said, “Damn. I wish I hadn’t spent $100 on that fire escape ladder.” There’s tight ass and then there’s just plain stupid.

Since you’ve probably already got a lot of the items I’ve mentioned just laying around the house (assuming you’re a pre-apocalypse reader), the basic stuff I talk about here is a pretty cheap EDC rig to assemble when you get right down to it. Obviously the extras or the alternate ideas will up the price, but the functionality in a survival situation is still more than worth your investment.

Altoids ® Tin $1.50
Gorilla Tape $2.97 a roll
Waterproof Matches $6.75
Starflash Signal Mirror $5.85
Emergency Whistle $8.00
Bic Lighter $1.50
Dental Floss $2.75
Streamlight Nano LED $10.00
MK5 Knife $20.00
Mini Compass $5.00
Ef Chlor tablets $10.00
Total: $74.32

The stuff I figure you already have or that you can bumb off a buddy includes:

If you do have to spend some money on that second list, I'm guessing $25 tops. You can't cram all of that into one Altoids ® tin (and it's not out of the question to have two), but you should pick what's going to work best in your situation -- now.

The new definition of procrastination? "Purina Zombie Chow."

Chapter 3: So What Are We Up Against?

As much as I hate to say it, everything that follows in this chapter is all technically "speculation" on my part. I'm not going to tell you that I have a friend who has a friend who has a brother-in-law who knows a guy who might work for a government think tank with initials nobody can figure out. Because even if that were true, which it is, you wouldn't believe me.

So, let's just pretend that everything we currently know is Hollywood's version of fictional portrayals of zombies that actually go back to the freaking Epic of Gilgamesh in 2500 BC — because nothing we've been talking about for that long could possibly have a shred of truth to it.

Okay. Now. For you people who are struggling with the math? That works out to 4,514 years. And for those of you who are going "Gilga-who?" It's the story Picard told Dathon in the "Darmok" episode of TNG. (If you're not a Trekkie, but you actually passed high school

English, it's also an epic poem from ancient Mesopotamia.)

That's right, folks. References to the re-animated dead go back more than 4,500 years. Some screenwriter in Hollywood did not make the whole thing up no matter how much you want to believe that's the truth. Denial might be comforting, but it won't get you where you need to be in this situation.

Even going with the movie version of what a zombie is going to be like, it's all a matter of picking your poison by this year's hunkie movie star du jour. The zombies trying to take Brad Pitt down in World War Z were some pretty vicious, fast-moving antagonists because a dude like Brad can't be taking on the wimpy undead. It's just not a manly man thing, and Angelina wouldn't like it.

Go rent the 1968 George A. Romero classic, Night of the Living Dead and you'll find slow, stupid, lumbering zombies that are dangerous because there's so many of them and they're so mindlessly relentless.

Sit through several seasons of The Walking Dead on AMC and you'll come to the conclusion that:

(1) zombies are always where you least expect them
(2) Rick really needs to get a Glock
(3) never trust what's inside a locked barn
(4) I want to be Daryl when I grow up
(5) somebody you like is always gonna get chomped
(6) who figured Season 1 Carol for a Season 4 bad ass

Sorry, couldn't help myself. Moving on.

Where is the real zombie apocalypse gonna land in the middle of all of those competing interpretations of what a zombie is and what it can and can't do?

I already touched on this a little in the section on "Why Is This Happening to Me?" One thing I do think is a given. When the zombie plague does begin, it'll spread like wildfire around the world in a very short period of time. Containment won't be possible, in part because the proliferation of the disease will be exponential. We're not talking epidemic. This will be a pandemic.

Every victim of a zombie attack becomes a zombie. I'm sure some pointy-headed math teacher could work a progression equation for us — in fact, they have, but I'm not supposed to know that — but I can give you the short answer.

We're screwed.

And this is not a matter of just waiting around for the undead to rot themselves into uselessness. Don't buy the "I'll just say indoors until it's over" line of reasoning.

Best estimates suggest that every single zombie has a "lifespan" of 3-5 years before they get too mushy, tattered, and just plain nasty to continue to pose a danger to the living.

Here's what I think we can know about the apocalypse and zombies in broad strokes:

- Those who are infected will spread the infection by unprovoked and spontaneous physical attack. The cause of the transformation from human to undead is likely a virus that is transmitted through the bite of an existing zombie.

- People who are wounded will likely run a high fever and be critically ill for some undetermined period of time before they die and then resurrect. It is not known if they are contagious during this stage of their transformation.

- The infected are driven by relentless hunger. I'm not sold on the whole "eat brains" thing. I think they'll take whatever body part they can get. Zombies are cannibals, not discriminating gourmands.

- Destroying a zombie's brain is, however, the only way to really put one down. You can blast his chest out with a shotgun and Ole Mr. Z will just get right back up and come at you again. If it weren't so damned scary, it would almost be awesome.

All the studies I couldn't possibly have read suggest that zombies have slow and shambling physical movements because their nervous systems no longer function correctly. Their nerves short-circuit every few seconds.

This looping malfunction makes the zombie's physical motions halting and uncoordinated. Think of them like a flickering light bulb. It keeps trying to go out, but it never quite gets there.

Not to mention the fact that zombies take the idea of muscle atrophy to whole new levels. Even though they seem to keep moving until they look like dried out pieces of beef jerky, zombies still suffer from greatly decreased muscle mass.

Don't convince yourself for a minute that a zombie can't be strong, but they can be overpowered if you keep your cool because no matter what Hollywood tells you, they're not fast on their feet and their reflexes are awful. Get over your initial revulsion and stay away from those snapping jaws and you can dance circles around one of these things.

Here's another popular myth a lot of people latch on to. "Oh, if the zombie apocalypse hits, I'll just find me an island somewhere and

I'll be perfectly safe." Okay. Work with me here. They're dead. Dead people don't breathe. Therefore, dead people can't drown. Come on. Do the math with me here.

Zombies don't have to swim. They can just walk in the lake and eventually walk out on the other side. They're not going to be strong enough to fight a good current, so getting washed downstream is likely, but sooner or later, they'll either get out in shallow water, or just get snagged on something on the bottom and gurgle while the fish have fun with them.

Never assume that any body of water, including shallow offshore ocean water, isn't also zombie infested. I wouldn't be going for any swims in murky pools if I were you, and do not be drinking that stuff without excellent purification — like boiling -- unless you're just hankering for a heaping helping of Cream of Zombie Soup. (More on water purification later.)

The undead can see and they track movement with their eyes, but primarily a zombie is drawn to sound. If nothing is going on around them, they kind of just stand there and rot quietly. Unless something attracts their attention and triggers their hunger, they have no motivation to do anything. All of these qualities can be used to your strategic advantage.

Three Things You Can Never Forget

Zombies are like cockroaches -- and thank God there are no zombie cockroaches because those nasty bastards are scary enough in their own right. My point is, if you see one zombie, expect all his little friends to show up for a play date sooner or later. Maybe you can't see them right now, but they are definitely there.

Getting yourself in a situation where you have to deal with multiple zombies is bad, bad, bad. You know that rule, "There is no such thing as an unloaded gun?" Well, with zombies, there is no such thing as just one. You are always outnumbered. This is now a fact of life.

Avoid confrontations with herds, hoards, whatever the heck you want to call them. In any equation where there's one of you and more than one zombie, the math is not in your favor.

Zombies feel no pain and are impervious to physical damage that would kill the rest of us instantly. They'll spew all kind of nasty, putrid fluids, but they don't bleed to death and they'll happily keep shambling along dragging a broken leg behind them until it's nothing but a bony stump.

Nothing but catastrophic damage to the brain puts them down. They can keep moving with a hole the size of a bowling ball blown clean through their chest.

And as if all of that weren't bad enough, they never get tired and they never get bored. If a zombie gets you cornered somewhere and has to beat down a door to get to you, he'll just keep clawing at that door until he get through. And the worst part? The noise he makes with all that mindless determination attracts his pals, so then he has reinforcements and pretty soon you're screwed by the massing effect.

Never forget these fundamentals of zombie physiology.

- They're rotting Energizer bunnies on speed.
- They exhibit single-minded determination and fixation because they feel no pain and experience no fatigue.
- In volume, they will overpower you. Pun intended.

Understanding what zombies can and cannot do is the foundation for all your decisions about how and when to confront and kill them, and when to stay far, far away.

Zombie Strategy 101

All strategies are based on available resources. If you’re holed up in a solid, defensible location with tools and raw materials at your disposal, you have a lot more actionable options.

Survivors stuck on the streets or wandering the countryside face limited resources and constantly shifting terrain and logistics as well as being completely at the mercy of prevailing weather conditions.

You have to learn to read the lay of the land and work with what you have. For instance, I get real ticked off at the people who will argue endlessly on discussion boards about the "best gun for the job." Dude. Seriously.

The best gun for the job is the one in your hand! Are you really gonna say to a snapping, snarling undead biker who is about ready to rip your head off, "Wait! Let me get my Desert Eagle Mark XIX."

(Yeah, yeah. I know you're jonesing for the gun talk. Fine. Are you out of your freaking NRA loving mind? A .50 cal hand gun? First off, it kicks like a mule with a bad case of hemorrhoids. If you're in L.A., the zombies in Pittsburgh will be able to hear the damn thing. Suppression is a joke. Where the heck are you gonna find the ammo? The dang thing is 15 freaking inches long and weighs just shy of 5 lbs. Get over your Dirty Harry self already. — And he carried a .44 mag anyway.)

There's no way I can possibly work through every strategic scenario with you. I can give you some basic information so you can start thinking like a survival strategist, because that's what you are now. This is not a video game. You have to make good decisions, or you won't be making any decisions at all.

So, to recap our discussion so far, here's the intel on zombies that we realistically have to work with going into this thing. These characteristics and traits are reliable givens for encounters with the undead.

- virulently infectious bites
- relentless hunger
- indiscriminate cannibalism
- physically slow
- uncoordinated
-

death by brain shot only
•
can't swim, but water is not an obstacle
•
drawn to sound
•
depend on external stimulus for motivation

How do we use this knowledge to our advantage? Well, for starters, don't get bit and don't think there are any "good" zombies out there.

- All zombies bite.
- All zombies will try to eat you.

You can't domesticate the undead.

Personal Shielding

The "not getting bit part" should be stating the obvious, but I'm trying to make a really serious point here. Avoiding bites is a proactive process.
When you have to go into an area infested with zombies, don't just protect yourself with the biggest baddest gun you can find. You need some kind of personal shielding.

Sooner or later, you will have to enter some location – on purpose -- where zombies are present. Hence the idea of purposeful preparation. At the very least go in with your extremities (read "arms and legs") protected.

Trust me. The new "greeters" at that trashed Wal-Mart chocked full of useful supplies will offer you a warm welcome — right before you join the ranks of the undead Walmartians for eternity.

(If that happens, and for the sake of what little bit of tattered dignity you may have left, I hope your tattoos are spelled correctly.)

Once you're over the initial panicked reaction and you're a little more used to the undead, you won't find it all that difficult to evade a single zombie when you can see it coming at you. In fact, they can be fairly predictable.

But if you come around the Mountain Dew display and run right into the undead Duck Dynasty crew? Chances are good one of those warmed over hillbillies will take a hunk right out of you for the simple reason that they took you by surprise.

Go into this kind of situation with as much personal shielding as you can rig and still stay mobile to avoid being taken unawares. It happens to everyone. The element of surprise isn't always something you can control, but trust me, your reflexes and reaction time will improve the longer you do this.

Personal shielding doesn't have to be prefabricated or all that elaborate. Even thick corrugated cardboard strapped to your forearms with duct tape can serve as makeshift gauntlets and could give you just enough time to fend off a zombie attack.

If you can swing it, actual riot gear would be a huge advantage, but it'll set you back better than $600 a suit. Now, for that you'll get hard shell panels over your back, chest, forearms, thighs, and knees with flex at key points. That includes a helmet and protective goggles.

It won't make you RoboCop, but you'll be close enough to live to die another day.

Hiding in Plain Sight

The strategy of hiding in plain sight is highly questionable and in my opinion way too risky. I think the undead can smell the living. Just trying to fall in with the hoard and mimic their uncoordinated shuffling won't let you blend in.

Even if you try to make yourself smell dead by rubbing zombie goo all over your body, you still have a beating heart. You're breathing. They just know.

I don't care how good it looks in the movies or on TV. Zombies are dead, their nervous systems are shorted out, they don't think, and they're not very fast, but they can spot their next Happy Meal a block off.

Whatever is left in them that constitutes instinct or a "mind" works well enough to tell the difference between fresh meat on the hoof and day old road kill. They don't go around eating each other. They're looking for something with a pulse -- you.

Use Sound Diversions

Thanks yet again to the movie industry, a lot of people expect to spend the entire apocalypse running and screaming with hoards of zombies chasing after them.

If that were true, you'd have the luxury of dropping dead from a heart attack instead of getting eaten. Go back and look at that list of zombie capabilities, Nimrod.

Zombies are attracted to sound, especially run-for-your-life girly screams. Done correctly? The apocalypse is gonna be your ultimate "quiet time." You actually want to avoid the whole running screaming thing because it makes you look like what you are, prey.

While you are doing do everything possible to move and live silently, the zombies are going to be stumbling around chasing down every rusty screen door banging in the wind.

Their behavior doesn't constitute high level hunting, but it's hunting all the same. Use that understanding of what they do and why they do it to your advantage.

If you need to be at Point A, which is completely surrounded by the undead, rig something that makes noise to get them interested in moving over to Point B.

Now. A warning. Every single zombie in the vicinity that hears that noise will start dragging their stinking selves over to see what's for supper. Do whatever you were planning to do and get out of there because you will have a herd on your hands in nothing flat.

Remember, one of the greatest threats zombies pose is sheer numbers coupled with tireless single-mindedness. You can deal with one or two if you're adequately prepared, but if 50 back you down an alley? Game over.

Build Obstacles

Regardless of where you ultimately settle down or for how long you plan on being there, build obstacles that capitalize on the fact that zombies are uncoordinated and lack the muscle mass or dexterity to perform fine motor functions.

Sure, a gang of zombies can push down a fence, but they won't climb it per se. The ones in back of the "line" may pile on top of the ones in front though. That's actually one threat scenario they got right in the World War Z scene when Jerusalem is overrun.

Zombies don't say, "Excuse me." They will trample right over one another and keep coming. If you let the bodies pile up, you have a problem. Fences are good, but it's essential that the perimeter be policed daily.
Yep. That's right. You have to clean up after yourself during the apocalypse. (And you thought Fido's poop bags were bad.)

I'll talk about this more later, but as soon as you smell a zombie, you'll know why taking out the garbage is not only a necessary chore for health and safety, but also something you'll actually want to do.

From just the standpoint of trying to achieve some new normal, looking at decaying zombies all day is well beyond demoralizing. Beyond that matter of post-apocalyptic aesthetics, however, there are still plenty of deliciously deadly illnesses and diseases you can pick up from parasites that have fed off those rotting corpses. Ditto for drinking fouled water.

Pitfall Traps

Pitfall traps are excellent, but they do require work on your part. You don’t need anything sophisticated for tripping up and capturing zombies. Just dig a hole deep enough that once they fall into it, they can’t get out.

There’s always the option of burying upright sharpened stakes on the floor of the pit, but since only a brain shot actually takes out a zombie, that’s just wasted work in my opinion — and it makes the pit harder to clean out.

The school of thought is divided on whether you cover the trap or not, but I wouldn’t take the chance of some latent instinct kicking in and the zombies going around.

Cover the opening with a thin overlaid mesh of branches and leaves. Remember, this is just camouflage to obscure the pit, you don’t want it to be able to take a human’s weight.

You do, however, have to consider what kind of human might fall through the trap: living or dead?

Unless you know for certain there are bad people in your area and you wouldn't mind catching them, too, mark the four corners of the pit and put up a warning sign. Zombies can't read, in case you hadn't figured that out already.

Clearly, there is one problem with this little bit of ethics. If you have managed to lay low and not betray your position to other survivors, the warning signs will give away the fact that you're in the area.

I'd rather risk letting other people know my whereabouts than be responsible for some poor schmuck falling into a pit of the undead, but I'll leave that one up to you and your conscience.

Cheval de Frise

Yeah, okay, I didn't really know what to call it. I had to go online and search for "sharpened stake defenses" because the only French I speak is followed by the word "fries." But that doesn't matter.

This cheval de frise thing has been around since medieval times when it was used as an anti-cavalry measure and it works great against the undead.

The one shown here is made out of a drilled central block of wood with crossed iron stakes. Doable if you have the tools, but you can just use a log for a central frame and lash smaller sharpened stakes to it to form the "x" shapes.

Put these around your perimeter and the undead will stroll right into the nice sharp points without batting an eye. Just like that. Zombie-ka-bob.

Of course you'll have to come along and put 'em down and pull 'em off, but better that than have your defenses breached.

This approach is much more effective than rolls of barbed wire, by the way, because the first zombies will pile up on the wire and make it solid enough for the second wave to make it over.

Also, you can get the materials to make a cheval de fries more readily than you can come by enough wire to really make a solid perimeter barrier.

Always think in terms of maximum return for your effort. The only man-hours you may have at your disposal during the apocalypse are your own. That makes sweat equity a whole lot more valuable and personal.

Watch, Look, Listen

Hopefully you're starting to get the idea. The more you observe zombies in action, the better you'll understand what they can and can't do.

SunTzu, the Chinese military strategist, best known for The Art of War, said,

“If you know your enemies and know yourself, you will not be imperiled in a hundred battles . . . if you do not know your enemies nor yourself, you will be imperiled in every single battle."

For the most part, surviving humans won't rely on offensive strategies. By definition, an apocalypse is more or less a defensive engagement.

I mean come on, war of attrition? Wearing down the enemy? Not gonna work with millions of undead shambling around. You can't exactly bleed an enemy dry when he doesn't bleed in the first place.

But getting conversant with basic defensive strategies can help you to start thinking like a savvy survivor. It's good to know about things like:

- The boxing maneuver where you "box in" your opponent and come at him from all sides. (You obviously will have to be part of a survivor group for this one to work.)

- Using a geographic "choke point" to concentrate the enemy in a confined area.

- Building fortifications and defenses, which we've just talked about.

And the one you should never think twice about using? Withdraw!

Know when to throw in the towel and back off. I call this the "we need a bigger boat" moment. If Quint had listened to Brodie in Jaws he wouldn't have been reverse sushi. I'm just saying.

Chapter 4: This is Not a Kum Ba Yah Moment

Now, assuming you're minimally prepared, let's talk psychology for a minute, which is about all the psycho babble I can handle before I hurl. This is specifically for you humanist types.

There will be no sitting around the campfire singing "Kum Ba Yah" with the zombies -- or probably anyone else for that matter. I didn't drink the Kool Aid on that one and neither should you.

Zombies Aren't the Only Enemy

I shouldn't have to tell you his, but here's the 411 on how it's gonna be, "The end of the world doesn't tend to bring out the best in people."

The zombies aren't going to be the only threat you're going to have to worry about. There will be plenty of living, breathing folks who are just as dangerous to your survival as the undead -- or more so.

That whole idea of man being civilized can go away really quick when push comes to shove. I know you probably think I sat around reading Guns and Ammo to get ready for this whole cluster . . . uh . . . crisis, but I've got some news for you.

Since I have every intention of being here to the bitter end, I figured out right quick that my biggest survival strategy was learning everything I could about possible disasters, including just how whacked my fellow survivors might be. So yeah, I've been reading, but not the kind of thing you might think.

Let's talk about two eggheads named Frey and Togler who wrote a paper called, "Interaction of Natural Survival Instincts and Internalized Social Norms - Exploring the Titanic and Lusitania Disasters."

Short version. Two big boats. Both went to the bottom. Lots of people died. Who went down with the ship and why? The numbers stack up pretty even:

- 2,223 people on the Titanic, 706 lived making for a 32% survival rate
- 1,960 people on the Lusitania, 768 lived, which is a 39.2% survival rate

First thing the profs did was arrive at a "reference group."

- Passengers on the Titanic age 35 or older with no spouses and no kids.

These people were like the red shirts on Star Trek. They were toast from the minute the ship hit the iceberg.

But two survivor groups really stood out on the Titanic. Women were 48.3% more likely to live than the reference group and first class passengers had a 43.9% better chance.

On the Lusitania? First class passengers were 11.5% less likely to survive and women were just 10.4% more likely to live. You know what was the real difference between the two situations and what really mattered the most in how people fared? Time.

The Lusitania went down in 18 minutes and people lost their freaking minds. It's a wonder anyone got off. The Titanic took 2 hours and 40 minutes to sink, long enough for "socially determined behavioral patterns to reemerge."

In other words, people remembered their manners.

You got a situation where the world falls apart slow enough for people to cope with it? Society is gonna hang together reasonably well. Everything goes downhill in an hour? People are likely to do damn near anything.

What are you going to do in advance to cope with that scenario? Get educated in a big damned hurry.

The Web is Gone. Deal.

If you have the time, start reading something other than "graphic novels." Get some useful information under your belt. Not just about field stripping an AK-47, but about what makes people tick, because once the apocalypse is upon us, Google will not save your butt.

That's right, sucker, no more Internet. If it's not gone already it will be before long.

Hopefully, you're ahead of the game because you have this book in your hands. Take some training courses ASAP — first aid, CPR, basic weapons, wilderness survival – or start working your way through the recommended reading list at the back.

Also, and you may not be expecting this one, you better get yourself something to believe in or at least to think about during those long, dark nights of the soul. I'm not talking religion necessarily, but if that's your thing, cool.

I like this old Roman dude named Seneca. He said it's easy to be a stand up, moral guy if you don't ever leave the house. Walk out the front door? Somebody will screw up your day. I stuffed a collection of Seneca's letters in my bug-out bag. Figured he'd be some company when I'm holed up somewhere.

Think about it. The day is gonna come when a book is your best friend even if you haven't picked one up in 20 years -- and I don't mean just a survival manual like this one.
Sooner or later, you will need something to remind you that you are still human and to give you a reason to keep surviving.

We're talking post apocalypse now. Maybe you haven't willingly walked into one since study hall, but libraries are good things. People have been teaching other people how to do stuff in print for generations and there are a lot of good stories out there. A book can be a lot of company, man. Don't dismiss the idea just because you hated school.

You already know you have a lot to learn. Find the educational materials you need – and the entertainment -- cause guess what?

If there's a Zombie Pride parade going by on the street outside your house, you have paid your last electric bill. Your favorite search engine is no longer an option for anything.

Keep a Notebook / Journal

Don't underestimate the value of keeping a notebook. If you want to keep a personal journal because you don't have anyone else to talk to, it can be a good coping mechanism. That's up to you. I'm mainly talking about a working notebook.

Once the apocalypse hits, you'll be under constant stress and in a hypervigilant state. That's exhausting and not very good for clear thinking. There are a lot of details you'll need to remember.

- Which stores have you already canvassed for supplies?
- What roads did you take to reach your current location in case you want to back track?
- What's your current inventory of supplies?
- How many zombies have you killed?

(Come on. You're going to keep score and you know it.)

If possible, I recommend having a waterproof notebook. Get something small and tough that you can shove in your pocket. Ditto on pens and pencils.

My favorite for field notes is the spiral Rite in the Rain Journal. It's $6.61 on Amazon or free if you're scavenging through a trashed stationary store.

(Zombie Apocalypse Bonus, guys. You'll never get in trouble for forgetting Valentine's Day again.)

The Rite in the Rain notebooks (32 lined sheets) will pretty much take anything. I've seen people write in them in a pouring rain. The same company makes an all-weather pen for $20 that looks a heck of a lot like a Fisher Space Pen (also $20). Your pick between the two, and the refills last a long time. Make sure these items are with your cache of supplies for long-term survival.

Also store any notes you take during your training and preparation that will be of use to you as a source of reference in the future -- but obviously keep this kind of thing in a compact form.

I'm not suggesting you run from zombies driving a Bookmobile. Every single thing you decide to put in your emergency supplies has to be there for a reason and has to have purpose.

Chapter 5 : Next Order of Business. Guns.

Yeah, yeah. I know, Rambo. You would have made this the first order of business, but truth is, most people think about running first. Then they finally get tired of running and realize they're gonna have to stand and fight at some point.

With that in mind, I will always hold to the wisdom that the best gun for the job is the one you have in your hand. That's going to be your only choice if you start looking for a weapon after the apocalypse hits.

Then my advice to you is to try to find something you're familiar with and can handle. No exotic calibers. Go for something like a 9 mil or even a .22. You have to be able to find bullets. The ammo fairy isn't going to just magically replenish your supply.

But if you come across a .357 and it's loaded? Pick that bad boy up and conserve those bullets like the gold they are until you either find more or locate a replacement piece. Any gun is better than no gun at all. Period.

This “best gun” discussion can and does go on for fricking ever, but here's my ideal zombie weapons cache in a nutshell.

Ruger 10/22

For a primary long gun when I have time and I want to stay quiet, I'd go with a suppressed Ruger 10/22 outfitted with the BX-25 x 2 for a total 50 rounds.

That'll take care of human threats and zombies. It's a super reliable weapon in all conditions and has pretty much been the .22 of choice for half a century.

Pump 12 Gauge

Now, for close quarter dirty work, there's nothing to replace a pump action 12 gauge. If you're dealing with bad people, just the sound of a shell getting racked into a riot gun is enough to make most folks stop and think. Since zombies don't think, just start blasting.
Good thing about your standard pump 12 gauge is they almost never jam and they'll

clear a room like a hot knife through butter, especially if loaded with double 00 buck.

If you've never fired a shotgun, the kick will surprise the hell out you. Best case scenario, you'll spend some time on a tactical range and get a feel for the weapon.

If not, plant your feet and brace yourself, but don't go completely rigid. Anticipate the recoil and take it into your body.

AK-47 Variant

For engagements out in the open when stealth doesn't matter or is not an option, an AK-47 variant is your best choice.

Why? Ammo is plentiful. The AK is so damned user friendly, kids in Afghanistan break them down and put them back together without missing a beat.

And this is one gun that will keep firing when it's absolutely filthy. It's so reliable you can even lubricate it with motor oil in a pinch.

Glock 17 9mm

For my sidearm, I have to go with the 9mm Glock 17. Remember that trashed Wal-Mart scenario? The shelves will be piled with 9mm ammo. Ditto for the country store with the sign that reads, "Beer, Bait, Ammo, and Prom Dresses."

This is roughly a $500 automatic. If you've never fired a gun in your life, get to a range, get an instructor, and go every day until you can hit what you aim at.

Complete Newbie in the Ruins

If you're balancing this book on one knee and staring at the Glock on the other? Well, we're going to assume it is a Glock because there are so many out there.

If you took the gun off a dead cop, I'm ready to lay money it's a Glock. Regardless, the principles are pretty much the same for all automatics, so just read what I have to say and work carefully.

The Glock has a safe action system and three safeties, so it's not gonna blow up in your hand or anything, but you do need to evaluate what you do and don't have in the way of firepower.

First off, hold the barrel of the gun pointed away from you and look for the button under the trigger that will eject the magazine from the butt of the gun. (If you're really a total newbie? The magazine is the part that actually holds the bullets.)

Press the button and drop the clip into you hands. Examine it to see how many rounds (bullets) you have. There are numbers on the back of the clip that will tell you. When you are ready to put the clip back in the gun, the numbers face toward the back of the grip.

Having the clip out does not mean the gun is unloaded. There could still be a round in the chamber. Still holding the gun away from you, take a firm hold on the grip with one hand. With your other hand, grasp the barrel just behind the front sight and push the slide backwards.

The chamber will open and if the gun is loaded, the round will eject. Even if no shell comes flying out, examine the chamber to make sure there's no sign of a shell. You should be able to see completely through the gun and grip where the clip would be.

Push the slide back and forth a few times. This will get you used to the motion and will absolutely confirm that the gun is unloaded.

You can lock the slide in the open position by engaging a small catch on the left side of the weapon when it's fully open and the chamber is visible.

(You need to know how to do this anyway for cleaning purposes.)

To make sure the gun is loaded, you basically reverse this procedure. Insert the clip in the handle. Make sure it clicks.

With the pistol pointed away from you, rack the slide back and forward again. There is now a live shell in the chamber ready to be fired. All you have to do is pull the trigger.
When you do fire, the spent shell is automatically ejected and a new one put in its place. The gun will keep firing until it's empty,

at which point the slide will lock itself in the open position.

Eject the clip and either reload it, or insert a fresh clip into the butt. Release the catch or manually close the slide. Remember, as soon as the slide closes, a bullet is in the chamber and the gun is ready to fire.

There is no manual safety on the Glock, which is yet again another source of endless gun enthusiast debate. What the Glock does have is a safe action trigger.

Look closely at the trigger. You'll see a little sort of blade jutting slightly forward out of the middle of the curve of the trigger.

Unless you have a full grip on the trigger and that blade is fully depressed, the gun won't fire, which protects against accidental discharge.

If you're not holding a Glock, there may be a manual safety, likely on the left side of the gun when it's pointed away from you. It will just be a little slide switch that's flush with the body of the weapon. If it's engaged, you won't be able to open the slide or pull the trigger.

Basic Gun Safety

I'm gonna give you some of the basic rules of gun safety, but they don't all apply in the middle of the zombie apocalypse. Now, getting ready for it all to go to hell? Yeah. Do this stuff.

- Always keep the gun pointed in a safe direction. The idea is to shoot the bad guy, not yourself, genius.

- The gun should always be unloaded when not in use. Uh. No. Not when there are zombies in the street. Better preparedness variation. "There is no such thing as an unloaded gun." Treat every gun as if there's a live round in the chamber at all times.

- Be sure of your target and what's behind it. Always a good idea, but if you're shooting into a moving herd of zombies and take down two with one shot? Score!

- If the gun doesn't fire when you pull the trigger, you may have a jammed shell. Try to clear the weapon. With an automatic, for instance, manually rack the slide. If you can't clear it and you have no proper tools, you may have to discard the piece, but definitely use extreme caution. It could go off at any time.

- Wear proper eye and ear protection. Yes on the range, not necessarily practical in the field -- although a good set of tactical sunglasses is never a bad idea. If you have a choice, go with amber lenses. They maintain natural colors in your environment.

- Be sure the barrel is free of obstructions before firing. Absolutely do this one, especially if you're out in the rain and muck. Do not let that barrel get plugged up. You'll not only blow your own hand off, but you may destroy the only weapon you have. If the Internet is still up and running, search for "gun barrel exploded" and look at the images.

- Don't alter or modify the gun -- unless you have a lot of experience with firearms and you know exactly what you're doing. For instance, if you find a long-barreled shotgun and have a hacksaw, I can totally see sawing it off. Easier to carry and it makes for a much deadlier field of fire at short distances.

I'm certainly not going to suggest that you shouldn't run while carrying a loaded gun. I'd just sound like your mother at the 4th of July. "Don't run with that sparkler! You'll put your sister's eye out!"

I will say, when you have to move fast with a weapon in hand, keep a good grip on the piece and make sure the muzzle pointed away from your body and away from the body of any living breathing person in the area. Nobody wants to be collateral damage because you tripped over your own feet.

Target Practice and Gun Handling

If you are learning all of this post-apocalypse, you can't be wasting ammunition or making a lot of racket with target practice. Here's a few basic tips:

- Do NOT do all those idiotic gangsta moves.
- Two hands on the gun.

- Don’t point. Sight down the barrel and aim.
- Try for the center of a living human.
- Go for the head shot only on a zombie.
- Exhale as you squeeze the trigger. Don’t jerk.
- Be prepared for the gun’s recoil.

If you are using a shotgun, don't fire from the hip. Shoulder the weapon firmly. If you don't, you'll land on your ass and you might not have enough time to get back up.

Ideally you'll be able to acquire good gun training in advance of the apocalypse and learn how to clean and maintain your weapon.

Very Basic Weapons Maintenance

I'm not trying to put together a field manual for firearm use, so I'm not going into field stripping and cleaning in any great detail.

My best advice is to acquire your weapons before the world goes south, become proficient with those guns in particular, and intimately familiar with their maintenance and construction.

Stockpile your ammo and cleaning supplies and take proper precautions to secure everything under lock and key. People will want to take what is yours. It's a given.

If it's post apocalypse and you know nothing about taking care of a gun, keep the weapon dry and dust free. Make sure no debris builds up in the barrel, which you can clean with a cotton patch coated with a little 3-in-1 oil or a similar product. You want a lightweight oil. Even WD-40 will work.

Draw the oiled patch up and down the inside of the barrel tucked into the slotted end of a cleaning rod. Wipe the area around the gun's action. Make sure all parts move smoothly and freely.

Don't go crazy with any over application of oil. Get too much on a gun, and the oil will just trap dirt and gunk instead of prevent rust.

And please tell me I don’t have to mention that the gun should be unloaded before you start cleaning?

Can You Pull the Trigger on a Zombie or Human?

God. I hope so, or you're dead meat walking.

Other Weapons

Let's face it. Anything that can turn a zombie's brain into mush and stop the thing from ripping your throat out is a viable weapon. You can use everything from a shovel to a sword so long as it gets the job done.

I would caution staying as far out of the zombie’s reach as possible. If your choice is between say a rolling pin and a hoe, go with the hoe.

If you're already proficient with another standard form of weapon, like crossbows, which get mentioned a lot in zombie apocalypse literature, then by all means, use what you're good with.

If you can't find a weapon of any kind and are basically wandering around defenseless, I'd strongly recommend avoiding other people until you're sure they're on the up and up.

As for protecting yourself from the undead in the interim, use the longest, sharpest, pointy thing you can find. Otherwise, follow a strict policy of avoidance and non-engagement. I'm sorry to tell you this, but defenseless people aren't going to last long in this new reality.

For those of you with black belts in this or that oriental discipline of Tai Kwan Kick Ass, forget hand-to-hand combat with anything that isn't breathing. Kick a zombie in the face and be prepared to lose a foot . . . and then an ankle . . . and then a knee . . .

A Word About Multi-Tools

A Leatherman isn't exactly a weapon, although it can certainly be used to make one, even if it's just sharpening a stick to make a primitive spear. I'm a huge fan of multi-tools and I really don't want to go into the apocalypse without mine.

Yeah, the model I carry set me back around $75, but here's what I got for my money:

- wood / metal file
- diamond-coated file
- large and small bit drivers
- large screwdriver
- needlenose and regular pliers
- scissors
- ruler
- wire cutters and wire stripper
- bottle and can opener
- clip-point and serrated knives
- lanyard ring
- Phillips and flat tip eyeglasses screwdriver

- saw
- Phillips #1-2
- screwdriver 3/16"

Maybe walking around in the normal world with that thing on your belt is just for show, but in the apocalypse, that's a heaping helping of multi-tool survival love. And really, do you care what other people think about what you carry on your belt?

When it comes to working equipment, I think a good solid multi-tool absolutely qualifies as a vital every day carry and I highly recommend that you acquire one and take it with you. When it comes to real return on your investment, this is one preparedness tool that will always be useful regardless of your setting or circumstances.

Chapter 6: A World Without Electricity

When things start to go bad, it'll be a gradual descent downward through new and progressive levels of bad. Have fun with that, because you won't have much of a choice. Nobody is going to snap their fingers and make it go away.

For a while, some of the features of regular life that keep you lulled into that nice fatal state of complacency will keep on working, but the first really big one to go will be the one we rely on most -- electricity.

This means you have two choices, learn to live in a world without power (which you will have to do eventually) or learn how to generate your own. It's typical for people to think, "Oh, I'll just get a generator." Fine if you can find the gasoline to keep it running, but those things make a lot of noise. Remember the basic equation?

- noise + zombies = a world of hurt2

My initial advice in regard to power is this: Don't ever pass up an opportunity to scavenge batteries, even if you don't have an immediate use for them. You can never have too many AAs. You have no idea how many things run on those little suckers. Eventually batteries will no longer be an option, but use'em while you can find'em.

Batteries 101

If you're like most people, you've always bought batteries, used them up, and tossed them. Way to go! You have done your part to kill the planet, moron. If that zombie beating on your door right now turns out to be running on nickel and cadmium, you screwed your own pooch.

The Basics

All batteries lose power over time and there's not much you can do about that. Depending on the length of time from the day the global plug was pulled, the batteries you find will be good for 2-3 years. After that, it's lights out.

Dying a slow death on the shelf may also mean your stored batteries will become "leakers." Here's the short Wikipedia version of why good batteries go bad and spew disgusting corrosive crud all over the place:

"As batteries discharge — either through usage or gradual self-discharge — the chemistry of the cells changes and some hydrogen gas is generated. This out-gassing increases pressure in the battery.

Eventually, the excess pressure either ruptures the insulating seals at the end of the battery, or the outer metal canister, or both

In addition, as the battery ages, its steel outer canister may gradually corrode or rust, which can further contribute to containment failure."

Deal is, you have one "leaker" the residue can spread to all the others, so check your stores frequently and get rid of the proverbial bad apples.

Rechargeables

The best rechargeables for apocalypse preparedness are the eneloops by Sanyo. They have Ni-MH Low-Self-Discharge chemistry, which translated into English means you can recharge them about 1,500 times.

Totally smokes the competition and there's no memory effect, plus they only lose 8% charge per year when stored.

Don't even think about getting a hand-cranked battery charger. Save your strength for fighting off zombies. Use a lightweight multi-purpose solar charger like the Goal Zero 41022 Guide 10 Plus ($120). It'll handle triple and double A batteries, measures just 6.5 x 9.5 x 1.8 inches, and weighs 1.2 pounds. With solar panels, however, remember the negatives:

- They don't work at night. (Duh.)
- Ditto for under cover.
- Solar takes time.
- Rainy days and Mondays get them down. (Well, okay, not Mondays.)

The point is, to be really effective, solar panels need 2-3 hours of direct sun. That means you have to stay in one place, zombie free for 2-3 hours on a bright sunny day. Getting everything all lined up for a perfect charge won't always be easy.

What I like about the Goal Zero is that the onboard battery stores some power if you can drain it into something else via a USB cable, and there's an LED light that will burn 150 hours per charge. Folded up, the whole thing is about the size of a regular book. That at least gives you a little more freedom to pick and choose your charging times and take advantage of spontaneous clear moments.

Really super serious about solar power and convinced you cannot live in a world without your laptop because you just will write the great American zombie novel? Okay, dude. You go drop upwards to $500 on a Goal Zero Yeti 400 Solar Generator and juice it up with a solar panel (not included).

Dang thing weighs 29 lbs. but it'll store enough power to top off a laptop up to 5 times. Of course, you'll have to find a zombie-free zone and as much as 52 hours of sunlight to accomplish that, but hey, I do like an idiot optimist.

They All Wear Out Eventually

The kicker is that all these commercially manufactured battery and power solutions will eventually run out and replacements will be impossible to find.

There are other ways to generate, store and direct power. Some variation on a water batteries will probably be your best really long-term bet, but you'll need copper and zinc strips to make that kind of thing happen.

(Remember what I said about learning everything you can before the apocalypse? This is the kind of project you should put on your homework list. Keep studying right up to the moment the zombie Avon lady rings your front doorbell.)

The Power of the Potato

I'm not an electrical whiz and we have other things we need to talk about, but I want to show you just how far outside the box you need to be thinking. You can light a room for a month with a potato -- and eat the damn lamp when push comes to shove.

Okay, yeah, I know that sounds ridiculous, but to generate power you need to facilitate a chemical reaction that creates an electrical current that can be directed through available wires. Believe it or not, you can do that with a potato.

Round up a big spud, a couple of pennies, two zinc-plated nails, three pieces of copper wire, and a little LED bulb.

Cut the potato in half and make a small cut in each one so you can slide the penny in there.

Wrap a piece of copper wire around each penny several times and stick the pennies in the potato with the wire dangling out.

Take the third wire and wrap it around one of the nails, then stick the nail in one half of the potato.

Take to the wire connected to the penny that's dangling out of the half of the potato you stuck the nail in and wrap it around the second nail, which you will then stick in the other potato half.
Connect to the two remaining loose ends of copper wire to the light bulb and it will light up thanks to the "salt bridge" the potato creates.

Two cautions:

- Be careful handling the wires, since there will be current running through them.

- Don't do this near an open flame or a strong heat source since you can get some hydrogen outgassing.

So why did I just take the time to type out a seventh-grade science fair experiment? To prove to you there's always a way. Remember what I said back in the beginning. Everything is a tool. Doesn't matter what it used to do. What can it do for you now?

Initial Emergency Lighting

While you're gathering advance supplies, get yourself a hand-cranked and solar-powered combo unit. That will give you a flashlight, a radio, and a charger for USB devices all in one package.

Granted you won't be making any cell phone calls, but being able to see photos on your iPhone of what your life used to be like will either drive you nuts or keep you going. Six of one, half a dozen of the other. Your call.

There are numerous models out there (thank you Hurricane Katrina), so take your pick. Most fall in the $30 to $50 price range. The world is a whole lot scarier without light and zombies don't sleep.

You'll also want a headlamp like the Petzl Tikka XP2. It's a little pricier than others at just shy of $60, but the maximum beam length is more than 200 feet and the burn time is 190 hours on a AAA battery.

You get three continuous lighting modes and a couple of strobes, but the real bonus is the red LED to preserve your night vision. Dang thing even has a 100 decibel whistle and its waterproof.

Chapter 7: Water and Food, Short and Long Term

Right out of the gate there will still be plenty of bottled water you can get your hands on. Don't drink anything else. There are walking corpses all over the place.

You know they can't swim, but they can dang sure marinate in every open source of drinking water you might find. Long-term, plan on capturing rain water and doing everything you can to purify water from all other sources. Don't assume any body of water is uncontaminated.

Water Purification Options

There are several options for really lightweight on-the-go water purification beyond actual water purifying tablets like the ones I talked about in the chapter on your Altoids ® survival kit. This first one is pretty good, but it does need batteries, which you already understand will become more and more problematic over time.

That being said, a SteriPen Traveler while a little pricey at $50, is really compact (about the size of one of those little 5-hour energy drink bottles) and the tapered end will fit into narrow-mouthed bottles.

So if you empty out a bottle of water, you can fill it with water from another source and purify it with the Steripen. The whole package weighs 5.7 ounces with the necessary four AA batteries in place. It's basically a UV light that's good for 3,000 water treatments.

I'm also a big fan of the LifeStraw Personal Water Filter for $20. It's a little bigger (8.8 inces long), but it will filter out 99.9999% of all waterborne bacteria and 99.9% of all protozoan parasites.

The LifeStraw gets rid of contaminants down to 0.2 microns and will clean up 264 gallons of water without any chemicals. It really is designed just like a straw, so you drink straight out of the filter.

Of course, tablets like Potable Aqua Water Treatment Tablets are the old tried and true standard. You do have to have something to hold the water to treat it, but the tablets only set you back about $6. They also don’t take up a lot of room, which is a plus.

The tablets are really just iodine, which primarily targets Giardia lamblia. Since we really don't know what bug will cause the zombie apocalypse, I'd go for the broadest based water purification method possible.

When you manage a quasi-permanent outpost, even if it's right by a running stream, I'd still recommend boiling all drinking water. You can never be sure what's in the water upstream or be 100% certain that the movement of the water is enough to protect you.

As part of the Rule of Threes, you can't survive more than three days without water. Worry about what you're going to drink first. It'll take you a good three weeks to starve to death.

Don't underestimate how much weight you're packing on when you try to carry water. You're looking at 8.34 pounds per gallon and at minimum your body should have about two quarts a day. In extreme heat though, you may lose half-a-gallon a day in sweat alone. (If you're racking your brain to remember, there are four quarts in a gallon.)

Rediscovering Fire

Notice that in the Altoids ® survival tin chapter I mentioned several items that could be used for tinder, like alcohol pads and cotton swabs. We included a Bic lighter (which can still be used as a fire starter once the fuel is gone because the flint will still spark) as well as waterproof matches.

With patience, you can even direct sunlight onto tinder with your signal mirror and get it to burn. But rub two sticks together like they do in the movies? Yeah, survivalists who really know what they're doing can make that work, but for most of the rest of us, that's just a ticket to blisters and high blood pressure.

There are a lot of cool little survival stoves out there and I'm not opposed to them in any way. The $70 MSR WhisperLite Stove is great, nice durable stainless steel and brass, burns all varieties of white gas, but seriously, do you really think you're going to be hanging out at Camping World and getting refills? Let's dig a little deeper and find our inner caveman, okay?

It's a heck of a lot easier to create a "stove" with an old coffee can and a pot with a smaller can. Hobos have been doing it for years. Just cut the bottom out of the coffee can and then make a rectangular cut on one side to serve as a door so you can keep feeding the cooking fire with small twigs and bits of wood. Also create a couple of vent holes.

On the other end, poke two holes on each side opposite one another so you can run some bent wire (even an old coat hanger will do) through to make a rack to hold your smaller "pot" in place for cooking.

Build a small fire in the base of the stove and put your pot on the rack. With a pretty decent little blaze, you should be able to boil water in about 5-6 minutes. If you're trying to warm something out of a can that's already cooked and you don't want to burn it, let your fire build up a nice bed of coals and then you have a more controllable heat level.

I'm not trying to turn you into the zombie Martha Stewart, but if you still have time, make one of these things and play around with it a little.

Hobo stoves are super easy and you can actually make some pretty decent chow this way. You're not dependent on specialized fuel and almost any "pot" will do, including your tiny little Altoids ® tin.

No water purifying equipment? Then boil water in a container over your hobo stove. Look. Until you get yourself organized and dig in somewhere, don't fricking over complicate stuff. The undead will do that for you.

Thing is, you have to drink and you have to eat. Accomplish that by the most direct route possible and worry about refinements to your apocalypse kitchen later.

Planning Emergency Food Stocks

You think the gun nuts can argue endlessly about what kind of heat to pack when the dead rise? Dear Lord. The foodies are worse.

We could just go down the MRE route and be done with it. Shell out $1200 and you have a year's worth of food with a 25-year shelf life for one person. Fine. Then what? Re-orders are not an option.

(Now, to get yourself started? A month's worth of MREs if you're flying solo may not be a bad idea. They're pretty cheap at $115 and having that much food on hand will let you get your legs under you and start really digging in and getting organized.)

But let's be brutally honest here. Most of us talk about buying supplies like MREs and we never get around to doing it.

I'm trying to talk to people who are really preparing and to people who are going to be stuck more or less reacting in the moment. Reacting is fine, but if you do it with good information, your reactions will hopefully be more intelligent and more effective than what the mob is doing.

We all lug stuff around with us. That's why I suggested a couple of packages of instant oatmeal to accompany your Altoids ® survival tin. The envelopes are thin and you don't need anything but water to make the stuff edible. In fact, hot tap water will do it if the electricity is still on.

By the same token, it's not a big deal to keep one or two energy bars or granola bars in your regular day bag inside a Ziplock ® bag. Just rotate them out every couple of months and you'll always have a little survival food with you.

But now we need to talk about what you store in big heavy-duty plastic tubs to either dig in at home or throw in the back of the SUV and bug out. Think high calorie load and long shelf life.

Certainly you do want some canned items if for no other reason that the empty cans themselves then become useful. But you also want to concentrate on staples like rice, beans, cornmeal, salt, and sugar. Pasta is excellent, as is peanut butter. Singly and in combination, you have a lot of high value nutrition options with this kind of item.

Most of this stuff can be kept in food grade plastic buckets you pick up at your local hardware store. A $5 gallon bucket will set you back for less than $10 and you can write on the outside with a Sharpie. Again, when it's empty, you have a useful container.

Why go this route? Let's take beans as an example. Beans lose oil as they age and they resist water absorption so they don't swell up. If they really get bone dry, you may have to grind them up to use them, but they'll still re-hydrate eventually and be usefully.

If beans are sealed really well and kept at or near 70 F, their shelf life is 8-10 years and they are dirt cheap. Pasta and rice stored under the same conditions will keep just as long and at least you have some chance of inflicting a little variety into staying alive. Also dirt cheap.

Starting to get the picture? I don't care what you serve on your post-apocalyptic table, just make sure that your emergency stores are kept well sealed, have high nutritional content especially in terms of calorie content, and have a long shelf life.

And you have to choose items you can afford to acquire now without negatively affecting your normal day-to-day life or you know as well as I do that you won't stockpile any emergency food at all.

How to Tell When Canned Food is Bad

If you're relying on canned (or jar) food you've stored or scavenged, realize it can always go bad. Don't eat anything from a container if:

- The can is bulging or the seal or lid is broken.
- There are any signs of rust or other corrosion.
- Anything is seeping or oozing out of the container or its lid.
- There are bubbles clearly visible and rising in the liquid.
- The food looks cloudy or moldy or seems mushy.
- The food smells bad.
- The jar or can spurts liquid the instant it's opened.

Now granted, there's a lot of irony to surviving just to die of botulism, but the spores are fatal. They can't be seen or smelled, so I really don't care how hungry you are – don't do it!

Never, ever risk eating food that may be spoiled and don't leave it behind for the next poor sap. It doesn't matter if you will never know that you protected someone else. It's still the right thing to do. Destroy the items, cinch your belt up a little tighter, and move on.

Seriously though, you cannot count on being able to scrounge canned food. That's not a survival strategy. That's frankly victim mentality. The whole idea of being a survivor is to retain control of your own fate, not to become a junkyard dog digging through the trash.

What About Edible Plants or a Garden?

There is no way I'm going to pretend to be a wilderness survival expert who can safely chomp on any old weed growing out there.

If you can, get ahold of a copy of A Field Guide to Wild Plants: Eastern and Central North America by Lee Allen Peterson and Roger Tory Peterson. I long ago stuck a copy in my bug out bag. That's definitely a situation where I need a book or I'm dead meat.

Frankly, I still have visions of myself getting chomped by a zombie while I'm down on my knees with a magnifying glass trying to decide if that weed is poisonous or not. Considering how many weeds I've poisoned in my life, seems like it would be a just end.

But if you really can dig in somewhere behind secure fences and you have decent soil and enough water to keep the plants alive, a garden is absolutely an option.

Packets of seed won't take up a lot of space in your cache of supplies and a supply of fresh vegetables will help you to stay healthier and even to store up food for the colder months of the year.

And yes, if you feel like you've just reverted to the days of your ancestors, you have.

And Then There's Hunting

Again, not Survivor Man, so I'm not going to make up a bunch of crap about hunting and snares and that kind of wild man of the woods stuff.

I used to hunt deer and I can do it again if I have to. What I'm about to say is yet again for the reader who has come across this book post-apocalypse and is just trying to make it one day at a time.

If you have a rifle and you can find game, of course you have to go for it – even if you do still have a PETA membership card in your wallet beside that Visa card you never have to pay off.

There. See. You can always find a silver lining. Okay, back on topic. I'll use whitetail deer as an example since they're so widely distributed across North America and are incredibly prolific.

For hungry newbie hunters, the important thing to remember is to aim just a little behind the shoulder and high. You'll either get a heart or lung shot. Both will work, but if you wound the deer and have to track it far, don't be surprised if one of the undead beats you to it.

In the absence of any good way to store or dry meat, just take the haunches. That's about all you'll be able to eat in one sitting and not be faced with anything going bad. Additionally, if I were you, I wouldn't be hanging around a supply of fresh blood any longer than is necessary.

When we were talking about the physical capabilities of zombies, I said there's no evidence they can smell the living. There is evidence they can smell blood and will be attracted to anything you kill while it's still warm and before decomposition sets in. All the more reason to take what you can carry and eat and get out.

Now, I'm sure there are plenty of hardcore survival types frothing at the mouth right now to tell me this is all screwed up advice. No disagreement here. I'm talking about life in a soon to be screwed up world -- even more screwed up than it is now.

If you're a pre-apocalypse reader and you have the time to cultivate wilderness survival and hunting skills, including tracking and trapping, do it! Wilderness survival and hunting are taught very well in a mentoring relationship. You can read all you like about tracking, for instance, but you need to see a trail to really learn how to follow it.

The same is certainly true for field dressing game and preparing the meat for both storage and consumption. I’m not saying you can’t figure these things out on your own, but a knowledgeable teacher will help you become proficient much more quickly.

Special Section: Bug-Out Bags Considered

Like all other survival topics, what should and should not go into any type of bug-out bag is a matter of heated and extensive debate. I wanted to include a list of potential items in this book, but with the strong caveat that these are just suggestions.

You have to do what's right for your personal circumstances. All of these items can either be stored as part of your supplies for a 72-hour plan or you can extrapolate to create stores for long-range survival goals. I'm just trying to get you thinking.

- Water. One gallon per person, per day.
- Water filters, purifiers, and potentially storage containers.
- Non-perishable, high calorie food that's easy to prepare.*
- Light sources with LED bulbs.
- Batteries as applicable per device or use.
- Alternative power sources (for example, solar).
- Hand-crank radio.
- Compass and maps.
- First aid supplies
- Specialized medications as needed.
- Sanitation and personal hygiene supplies.

- Multi-tool / cutting tool.
- Weapon(s) / ammunition.
- Fishing supplies.
- Cooking / dining implements.
- Good quality space blankets, not the cheesy single use variety.
- Supplemental clothing.
- Two-way radios if you're with a group.
- Manual can openers.
- Emergency whistle and/or signal mirror.
- Matches and/or other fire starting gear like a ferro stick.** Rain gear and/or tarp(s) or plastic sheeting.
- Tent. ***
- Duct tape and/or gorilla tape.
- Towels.
- Work gloves.
- Cutting and digging tools. (And scissors.)

* Three-day supply minimum, preferably two weeks or more.

** Here's the Wikipedia 411 on a ferro stick, "Ferrocerium is a man-made metallic material that gives off hot sparks at temperatures of

1,650 °C (3,000 °F) when scraped against a rough surface."

*** Or supplies to construct a shelter if you are working on your long-term stash of supplies.

Clearly this list can go on forever. One of the things survivalists do as a matter of course is plan and study, thinking through their supplies, keeping an inventory, adding and subtracting items as they envision new scenarios in their heads.

This isn't obsession, people, it's refinement, and it's a good thing. Preparing for the end of the world is not a mindless hobby. This is serious business requiring serious intention and real forethought.

Bear in mind there are levels of intensity and purpose with these bug-out bags, which is the generic term for various kinds of survival packs.

• An EDC or every day carry is the smallest survival pack and is intended to be with you every day. It can be in an actual case like an Altoids tin, or even just items you ensure are on your person daily.

- Go bags are essentially mission specific. If X happens, I have all the supplies I need to get to Y and function.

- A 72-hour bag in theory holds all the items you or your family will need to survive for three days.

- A get home bag is typically carried in your car or kept at your place of work. It has whatever you think you'll need to get you back home or to your primary base of operations safely.

- A vehicle bag is a variation on this theme and may also include tools to keep the car or motorcycle operational during a crisis.

- An office kit is get another variation of the get home bag, but with the intended purpose of allowing you to hunker down at your place of work in the wake of a crisis.
- An INCH bag means "I'm never coming home." It is typically the largest of all the survival kits and has everything you need to

start over. It is kept at a separate and secure location and is often described as a bug out bag on crack.

- Your cache or stash takes this whole idea one huge step farther. It's a hidden supply of equipment, weapons, food, and anything else you will need to live, start over, and even barter in the new post-apocalyptic "economy."

One thing is for certain, almost any level of preparation you complete before the zombie apocalypse begins will put you in an infinitely stronger position than the great mass of humanity that is about to get served up as hors d'oeuvres.

Another thing you might want to consider in putting your bags together. Choose packs that don't scream, "I have everything I need in this bag to protect myself and get through the apocalypse."

If you come charging out of your office with a camo pack slung over your shoulder dangling all kinds of canteens and the like, you are going to look like exactly what you are, a walking supply depot ripe for the looting.

If people realize that you have useful supplies, tools, food, and water, they will try to take those things away from you. Choose packs and bags that are low key and don't advertise their contents. You not only want to have the necessary supplies to bug out, you want to move through the panic as unobtrusively as possible. Being silent around the zombies is an essential skill, but at the same time, make sure you are virtually invisible to other humans who will take what you have and likely harm you and yours in the process.

Chapter 8: First Aid and Hard Choices

Look, I think we can all handle splinter removal, basic wound cleaning, maybe even snakebite. There are enough ex-Boy Scouts, weekend EMTs, and Discovery channel junkies wandering around out there to have most of that moderately nailed.

Great big major illnesses requiring sophisticated medical intervention, equipment, surgeries treatments? Uh. Yeah. Okay. Let me say this as gently as I possibly can. Make peace with your Maker.

For ordinary run of the mill stuff we all come down with just because we're still alive? The same way you never turn down the chance to scavenge AA batteries, leave no drug behind. If you don't know what the pill is, or if it's something like Lipitor for high cholesterol, don't bother.

Seriously? You think a zombie cares if your arteries are clogged? You're probably getting more exercise than you ever have in your life. Screw your cholesterol.

But your average run of the mill antibiotics like Keflex, Zithromax, or Erythromycin? Grab that stuff up in a heartbeat. Even a bottle of Pepto can save you from the potentially deadly dehydration that accompanies diarrhea if you get ahold of some bad food.

The worst thing that can happen to your health wise is a confrontation with a zombie that results in a bite. If that happens, what's next? Or is there a next?

Dealing with Zombie Bites

If a zombie bites you, you're infected. That's it. No theorizing. No guessing. No need for lab tests. No second opinion required. If the bite is to one of extremities (an arm or a leg), however, immediate amputation is an option. Anywhere else, and you will turn.

Of course, if amputation is attempted, then your challenge is surviving the shock and blood loss and managing to heal without serious infection or gangrene setting in -- not to mention how vulnerable you'll be to further attack while you're laid up. It's gonna be dicey as best and hurt like hell.

So what do you do if you get bitten?
Well, if you're in a group and anyone has even rudimentary medical knowledge, amputation may be viable since someone will be there to help you afterwards. If no one is willing to attempt the surgery, you won't have any choice but to let the subsequent fever run its course and be put down after you turn into one of the undead.

Self-amputation? Yeah. Most people don't have the chops for that, so that just leaves manning up and getting it over with.

The Ultimate in Self-Responsiblity

If you're bitten and you know you're going to turn, are you really going to ask somebody else to do the deed for you and then have to live with themselves? Not me.

It's one thing if someone is so bad off they're out of it or suffering. Then putting another person out of their present and future misery is the only decent thing to do.

But if a zombie chomps me and I know what's coming, I'd rather be in charge of my own exit than saddle somebody else with the chore or let myself become the next junior zombie scout on the block.

Look, I know a lot of people have moral qualms about suicide, but I think I have moral qualms about turning into a mindless cannibalistic ghoul. Maybe that's just me, but I think that trumps suicide any day. If there is an afterlife and I don't get in because I decided not to become a reanimated serial killer, I'm good with that.
So my advice is always keep one bullet in reserve, for yourself. If you're going to turn anyway, or if the undead get you trapped somewhere and there's no way out, a bullet to the brain will make sure you don't get chewed on and initiated into the undead frat party.

If nothing else, just think how much you'll hurt before you bleed out or die of fright. No thank you. Same reason I never took up lion hunting. I'm funny, but I have an aversion to being eaten.

If you're the vengeful sort and want to rig up some kind of explosive charge to try to take as many zombies with you as you can under those circumstances, I don't have a problem with that. Trouble is, you can't count on an explosion making sure you're dead enough.

Mortality isn't as cut and dried as it used to be.

No matter what else you have planned for your big exit, make sure the last thing you do is blow your own brains out. Do not be one of those losers who just doesn't get it and opts for some big dramatic exit like hanging yourself. If you're already infected, you'll just wake up a zombie wind chime.

Preventive Clean Up

One of the best strategies you can follow in the name of preventive health care post-apocalypse is just work the garbage detail. When you kill a zombie, dispose of the remains. They’re nothing but walking toxic waste dumps.

For one thing, zombies stink to the high heavens and it gets worse the longer you let them pile up. Then they start attracting all kinds of nasty insects, like flies, that pass along disease. Also, it's pretty demoralizing to be constantly looking at zombie road kill.

For practical reasons, however, letting putrefying zombies more or less seep into the water table and become part of the regular run off ensures water contamination and potentially plant contamination as well. You want to eat vegetables growing downhill from a stinking pile of zombie rot? Be my guest.

Burning zombie bodies in pits is probably your best option, but there are problems with going that route. Digging the pits is hard work and the smoke may attract more attention than you want -- most likely from other living humans who may or may not be friendly.

At the very least, get the zombie bodies out of your immediate area and at a decent enough distance from your camp or shelter that you're not living with the stench, the insect activity, and just the demoralizing effect of having to watch those disgusting things mold.

Controlling Your Stress Levels

One thing is a given. Life in the post-apocalypse world will be a hyper-vigilant existence. You have to find someplace where you are safe enough to get some sleep and just stand down for awhile. The effects of sustained long-term stress will hit you at every functional level:

Cognitive:

- Decreased memory capacity.
- Reduced powers of concentration.
- Poor judgment and decision making.
- Inability to see positives.
- Constantly racing, anxious thoughts and worry.

Emotional:

- Irritability, short temper, moodiness.
- Agitation and an inability to relax.
- Intense feelings of being overwhelmed.
- Deep loneliness and a sense of isolation.

- Severe depression.

Physical:

- Muscle / joint aches and pains.
- Nausea and digestive problems.
- Dizziness and vertigo.
- Rapid heart rate and potential chest pain.
- Susceptibility to infections.

Behavioral:

- Loss of appetite.
- Insomnia or sleeping too much.
- Self-isolation.
- Disinterest and procrastination.
- Drug and or alcohol abuse.
- Development of nervous, repetitive habits.

Now, clearly the world as we know it coming to an end is gonna be a little stress inducing. And some of the things on this list are necessary to stay alive. Complacency and inattention in a survival situation are bad things. But you will have to ensure adequate amounts of both physical and emotional rest or there is no way you can stay at the top of your game.

Politicians on the campaign trail say to never pass up the chance to go to the bathroom. As a survivor in a post-apocalyptic world, you should never pass up the chance to sleep, eat, get clean, or do something that will give you even a moment's pleasure or a hint of relaxation. That doesn't mean you completely drop your guard, but you do have to ease your finger off the trigger every now and then.

First Aid Reference Material

Again, if you are a pre-apocalypse reader and have the prep time, get a copy of The Survival Medicine Handbook: A Guide for When Help is NOT on the Way by Joseph Alton and Amy Alton. This is another vital reference to have with your end-of-the-world supplies.

Chapter 9: A History of Conflicts and Violence

Human conflict has been present since the beginning of time and with the current state of numerous international conflicts around the globe, it's easy to deduce that war isn't going anywhere anytime soon. In recent years we've since an increase in genocide, civil war, and international disputes ranging from territory disputes to conflicts over natural resources.

This isn't really all that different from other conflicts present in humanity's past. Early nomadic humans waged war in local areas throughout all the habitable contents through tribal warfare and were conducted with primitive weaponry. What began as hunting tools, like spears and heavy rocks tied to sticks in a crude version of a hammer, quickly became our first weaponry against our fellow man.

As the human population grew, so too did the groups of humans clustering together. Tribes grew into villages, villages into towns, and towns into cities. Man's capacity for engaging in disputes did not change no matter how great humanity's population grew or how many intellectual leaps we made. While we may have come to understand the movement of the solar system and how to achieve flight, our capacity for violence did not lessen.

So what changed? Why is the zombie apocalypse so much more likely now than it has been in eons past? The answer is simple and direct. We now have easier access to places that are geographically distant and higher technological resources to kill one another through the use of bio-weaponry.

Arriving at this level of technological advancement has been a horrifying road. Experimentation in human genetics and evolution really didn't take off until WWII, so in the timeline of our history, we've only been dabbling in human biological experimentation a short period of time.

It can be argued that the invention of the healing arts, a rather ancient practice that has been studied almost since the inception of mankind, was actually the true beginning of human experimentation. However, for the sake of this book, it is much easier to start with the beginning of human experimentation as it deals with ending human life rather than healing as it is more relevant to our study.

In the mid-1940s, the Nazis took human experimentation to a level of cruelty that far outstripped any human experimentation previously. Through the use of prisoners interned at concentration camps like Auschwitz, Nazi scientists ran many scientifically unethical experiments that largely had few merits outside of finding creative ways to kill their charges. They did however have goals in mind for the end goal of experimentation which included: helping German military personnel in combat situations through advancement of understanding of human physiology, the development of new weapons, aid in the recovery of military personnel who had been injured through observation of injuries purposely given to test subjects, and the advancement of the Nazi racial ideology.

Twin studies, bone, muscle, & nerve transplant experimentation, head injury experiments, freezing experiments to test human limits for hyperthermia, malaria experiments, immunization experiments, mustard gas experiments, sulfonamide experiments, sea water exposure experiments, sterilization experiments, poison testing, incendiary experiments, high altitude experiments, and blood coagulation experiments.

In the end, the Nazis did actually yield some fairly valuable, and unfortunately dangerous, data in regards to human life and we've only improved our understanding since then. Our understanding of blood borne pathogens, neuro-chemical instability, and immune responses have led to the development of some highly suspect chemical components including anthrax, cancer-causing chemicals like asbestos, and radioactive chemicals that mutate human beings on a cellular level.

The space race of the 1950s and technology race that is still going on today are leading to ever-more-complex methods of killing one another. With billions being spent in the areas of nuclear testing and even more being spent currently on bio-weaponry, it's only a matter of time before the use of bio-warfare erupts on a widespread level.

Judging by how the world handled outbreaks like the Ebola virus just a few short years ago, we are completely unprepared for what is to come. While there are procedures in place for the containment of highly dangerous bio-agents, which the CDC classifies as "red" agents, oftentimes agencies are slow to react in case they cause a wider problem with panicked civilians and governmental agencies are oftentimes far more worried about possibly inciting voter wrath than in protecting the world at large.

In addition, by bombarding our natural pestilence with antibiotics and harsh chemical treatments, we are forcing our bacteria, fungi, and viruses to evolve at an astronomical rate. If nature takes a turn and begins to infiltrate our bodies like the Ophiocordyceps fungus shoots spores onto an insect, we will all be in big trouble. You might have heard of this fungus before; it's the so-called "Zombie" ant disease which turns a normal ant into an unthinking being completely controlled by the will of a fungus. The distance between that type of parasitic fungus behavior and zombie behavior is minimal.

Added to the fact that scientists are viewing these types of parasitic behaviors as possible weaponry, humanity is much closer to the brink than the average person assumes.

Both nature and man seem to be conspiring to wipe out the human race. The question is, which will kill us first?

History of Bio-Agents Used

The use of bio-agents is prevalent in every aspect of modern society. It should be no surprise to anyone reading this book that everything from our food to our receipt paper holds some sort of added chemical that is absorbed into the human body. Human beings are being changed and mutated in small increments with every breath we take. It makes you wonder if there isn't some grand experiment that some mad scientist isn't running on the world at large.

There could definitely be many a chapter of poetic verse dedicated to the infiltration of chemicals into our modern society but that scope is far too large to cover. Instead, let's go over some very basic tactics in wartime that people have used throughout the ages in order to bring about their desired outcomes.

If we start from the very start of humanity in tribal times, it was a well-known fact that human beings kept together in poor conditions often developed illnesses. While ancient human beings may have expected prisoners to experience sickness and eventual death, they didn't know the mechanics behind this is so. However, it was very effective at keeping the enemy weak and killing off portions of the population through internment. This is the most rudimentary level of bio-agent use in warfare. You take a population and introduce an ill subject into the equation and simply wait for the illness to spread. It's crude and not always effective but it does get the job done for the majority of your cases.

Untreated injuries tended to get infected prior to the use of antibiotics. In ancient Rome, those who didn't get treated by a healer often ended up losing a limb to save a life or losing their life.

If we examine how Christian prisoners were treated during the age of the gladiators, we can swiftly see Rome using the same sorts of tribal tactics on their fellow man. Christians were housed in huge underground chambers during gladiatorial matches and even if they survived a bout or two, their injuries led to infection and eventual death.

In the 6th Century, Assyrians used a fungus introduced into well water to poison their enemies and incapacitate them in order to overrun their villages. Mongols used the bodies of their dead as weapons to use against enemies in the 12th century, knowing that dead flesh spread diseases.

It could be argued that this was simply a fringe benefit of allowing wounds to fester and rot but even on a rudimentary level, the outcome is the same. Allow an infection to go unchecked, all hell breaks loose in the human body. It's just that simple.

You might ask when the first time a people truly used bio-agents to attack, not just as a fringe benefit, but as a concentrated effort to spread infectious disease.

Our earliest knowledge of deliberate spread of bio-agents for the purpose of attacking another faction is probably during the Andrew Jackson presidency with the Trail of Tears. This rather sad time in American history has provided evidence that soldiers would deliberately distribute blankets known to have smallpox bio-agents in them in order to infect populations as they were made to walk from one end of the USA to the other.

This is the first time we can really see a deliberate effort to eradicate another species from the face of the planet simply through the use of tiny microbes that people at the time did not know about or truly understand. Even if they didn't know how people carried diseases, they knew that the diseases spread when exposed to other people who had them. This seemed to give human beings all the knowledge they needed to set us on the path of using bio-agents to cull populations and, essentially, weaponized bio-agents for use against enemy populations.

From there, the spread, pardon the pun, continued to grow. World War II saw the rise of mechanized bio-weaponry with the deliberate push of different methods of disease introduction via their concentration camps. Their actions were morally reprehensible but it did not mean that the rest of the modern world didn't use the knowledge gained from the Nazi experimentation to their benefit. The knowledge was used to expand bio-agent understanding.

The Nazis were not the only ones who were quick to figure out that bio-warfare was the way of future conflicts. The Allied forces during this time were also developing their own chemical and biological weaponry in preparation for the German assaults. Thankfully, those bio-agents were never used, however, they ended up stored in the knowledge bank of the involved governments, waiting.

Nuclear warfare put the use of bio-agents on the backburner for several years as scientists pondered whether this type of weaponry would really make the best weaponry in this new connected modern age. It only took a brief look at the science to realize that conquering nations did not want to leave a nuclear wasteland in their wake. It was a good final solution, but if the people doing the attacking wanted to preserve the land for future use and not cloud the world in endless smoke fields of radiation, they needed another solution. A better one.

The eighties saw the rise of the Cold War and with it fear of Nuclear attack. That wasn't all that was happening rapidly during the eighties. The rise of HIV and AIDS showed the world how easily large swaths of populations could be wiped from the world with a simple introduction of a virus.

As much as modern science was able to combat this modern plague, it couldn't completely eradicate it like it had managed to do with many other bacterial infections that were able to be treated with antibiotics. This gave governments the understanding that they were much better off using a biological agent than a large-scale nuclear attack. Human beings were much more fragile than buildings and machines.

Enter the nineties and two thousand with the antibiotic-resistant bacteria and the world develops some interesting new fears. Panic spreads, rumors start circulating the media, but it's all hushed because the government is able to contain the spread thanks to its CDC containment plan. These are just organic modern diseases.

Use your imagination. The governments of the world certainly did. They started thinking bigger, better, and more effective. Bio-warfare can spread fear, chaos, and devastation better than any bomb ever could because it could be everywhere and nowhere. They had their perfect weapon. They just had to figure out which bio-agent was the best one to use against their enemies.

Forbidden Research Made Possible

The answer to the question that scientists had been puzzling over since modern warfare began came from the most unlikely places. Popular culture, fantasy, and science fiction has given rise to the idea of a reanimated corpse, a zombie virus, an unstoppable force. With roots in both science, as with the fungus that takes over the brains of ants, and ancient voodoo practices of enslaving a human being in a shuffling, dreamlike state, the zombie was a hint of a biological idea that sparked the scientific imagination. If you think about it, all of the humanity worked together to give rise to the idea that a hands-free warfare option was not only possible but preferable to any sort of modern warfare. Terrifying isn't it? At this point, the idea of governments doing "zombie" experiments falls off the people's radar, a deliberate action by their part, no doubt. Hints of their involvement in the experimentation into zombie-like strains of bio-agents do pop up every now and then.

It's been a long-held belief that drugs like crack were first tested on low-income populations in an effort for the government to determine whether or not the drug was an effective form of treatment for pain as well as eliminate some of the people deemed "unfit" in society.

Enter bath salts, a designer drug that became intensely popular for several years during the early 2000s. Everything seemed to be just fine for a while, a fun drug that entertained youth and then, of course was subsequently banned once the media caught wind of it. Of course, that didn't mean that bath salts went away.

Something highly interesting did come up though: The world's first zombie killings.

A Chinese immigrant in 2009 beheaded and then ate a man's face on a bus in Canada. Authorities said he was making "animalistic noises" and was "unresponsive" to any outside stimulation while consuming his victim. In 2012, he reported that he thought the person was "an alien" but no further explanation was given other than a blanket mental health statement from supposed experts. This might have been our first zombie experiment wrought by the Chinese.

May 26, 2012. Rudy Eugene attacked a homeless man and partially ate the man's face before being shot and killed by the police. The homeless man did survive but he was severely maimed. The drug did wear off eventually and the man regained his sanity but the damage had been done.

The authorities learned two things from this event: People could be reduced to mindless man-eating machines but it wasn't permanent and it wasn't effective at spreading the disease. They needed something better.

Fast forward to 2016. Two zombie slayings in less than six months. One is a college fraternity student who killed and devoured an elderly couple. The other Washington Mall Shooter who, after killing and injuring dozens of people at a mall, was in a zombie-like state when he was arrested.

If you look worldwide, you will see other incidents that resemble the same pattern. A person who doesn't normally indulge in "drugs" is suspected of drug use. The drug is often one that people have never heard of or heard very little of. Nothing is confirmed. Suspects are usually of low intelligence or easily led. Interesting test subjects, don't you think?

Following the timeline, you can deduce that the zombie-like qualities of these attacks are growing in intensity. It begs the question, are the drugs getting worse or are the bio-agents getting better?

Let's just assume scientists have developed the zombie bio-agent. They might have even figured out how to spread it but their options are endless. Let's take a look of at them, shall we?

Bacteria like anthrax can be spread by depositing it in baby powder and then sent via the mail. It can also be aerosol contained and spread via the air. This method of dispensary would be as simple as dosing a populated city with powder or air released via a high-density gas. Adding a bio-agent to a similar agent of dispensation and you have an air-born zombie apocalypse.

Another effective way would be poisoning the water supply via the agent. This one is a bit harder than the first method because it has to be capable of withstanding water treatment. However, if manipulated the correct way, it would expose the entire city population to it via the drinking water, shower water, laundry, etc. Add absorption through the skin and you have a tailor-made zombie apocalypse.

Animals are actually a common way for infection to spread. Think of mad cow disease and its insanely high mortality rate in humans. Imagine a way to infect the food chain. It may be months before the authorities even figure out where this type of disease comes from. Rural regions would be particularly devastated since their food supplies are limited.

Cross-species contamination would make an animal infection even better for the infection rate. If the zombie pathogen could pass from animal to animal, the rate of infection would grow from ingestion from a single animal to a multitude of animals with minimal work. This manipulation of genetics is fairly simple to reproduce in a lab setting, making the likelihood of infection all that much higher.

The classic method of delivery and probably the next step after the initial infection is the spread. Bites. Yep. This is where your infection will most likely come from. Saliva is the best transference method but there is also blood, which would come from any number of methods, most likely open wounds and sores.

This is just a few of the ways the bio-agent can be used to infiltrate populations. With some of the best minds in the world working on this, the possibilities are indeed endless.

We've already discussed why the development of a zombie virus is not only probable and possible but also very likely due to its effectiveness. Let's get into the nitty, gritty reasons of why countries might consider doing something so incredibly risky and immoral for the sake of war.

The ban of nuclear weaponry is one of the biggest reasons countries are getting into the development of biological weaponry. Since we are now considered a global entity with economies entwined to a degree that one's collapse would lead to the decimation of another, a full out nuclear war would not only be viewed as unfavorable by other countries, it could lead to the outright hostility from other countries affected by the economic impacts.

This could be detrimental to the attacking country. Other countries could be united under the purpose of retaliation and the attacking country could have even worse inflicted on them than if just the primary target had retaliated. Economic sanctions could be the first step, leading to economic hardship. Aggression could lead to a multi-front war, something WWI and WWII have both shown us is not the ideal.

No country likes bad press and the world would see this as an overkill, regardless of the reasons behind the attack. Using a nuclear weapon is a bit like bringing a gun to a knife fight. Everyone tends to see it as disrespectful and over the top.

Even if you leave out the element of nuclear aggression, all-out warfare is still seen as overly aggressive by modern standards. First world countries are now on the path where they see military aggression as a last-resort option and countries who use it as only one step up from complete anarchy. Losing face and credit like that is only good if you want to destroy the whole world. If you want to have any allies after the fight, this is not the way to keep them.

Shadow wars are the only way to truly fight a war in the modern age. Shadow wars eliminate the need to involve other countries because they are, in fact, invisible. No one knows where it comes from, only the end result. Pass or fail. Even if you fail, no one will know, meaning the entire country saves face.

Shadow operations lead to the necessary development of sneakier means to get at your enemies. This leads to the development of sneakier forms of warfare. Zombies are the ultimate untraceable solution to the shadow wars that inevitably happen in the modern era. There ends up being no one to intimidate, no one to confess secrets. There is only an unstoppable force with no morality

and no regrets. The risk is actually minimal and the potential payoff exceptional.
The invasion takes manpower and it takes a frontal war. Zombies allow for a war without a single hour of manpower on enemy soil. Find the right release mechanism and infect a single member of the population. This singular infection can span thousands of people. Welcome to having an entire army at your disposal without a single solitary risk factor involved in the origin country.
Brains! Brains! Brains!

Zombie behavior is often characterized by a number of fantastic descriptors. Moaning "brains" and shuffling around aimlessly is the earliest behavior that stereotypical zombies exhibit. Biologically as well as weaponry wise, this isn't a very effective way to create an army. Brains aren't the easiest organ to get to and while the protein-rich substance may be particularly useful for a protein-feeding bacteria or protein-driven viral strains but the easiest protein feed is the flesh and organs that are easiest to reach. Like we've stated before, not an effective way to create an army.

Assessing the biology is a much better indicator of behavior. Since there are several avenues of how the zombie will behave based on the type of infection and possibly pre-programmed behaviors makes it even more interesting. Let's talk zombie types.

Infectious, psychoactive bacteria or viruses are designed to kill every part of a person except the cerebellar functions. The easiest parts of the brain to activate is the primal parts. Aggression centers in the brain are easy to trigger. Directing that aggression toward their fellow mankind would create a highly aggressive subhuman that would attack basically anything that moved. This would extend toward nonhuman entities and humans alike. This type of infection would be effective in population dense areas.

We already have this type of bacteria in existence in Lactobacillus rhamnosus (JB-1). This psychoactive bacteria affects brain chemistry and relevant behavior. By stimulating the vagus nerve via the central nervous system originating in the gut bacteria, this bacteria effects the emotional centers of the brain. Manipulating the bacteria to amp up certain characteristics is just a measure of selective breeding. This could be performed in almost any lab and the trick ends up being making the bacteria resilient enough to resist antibiotics or other pathogen combatants. Again, doing this is a lab is the most effective method of performing this.

Targeted furious rabies strains would be another quite effective delivery system and a good indicator of behaviors. Rabies causes inflammation of the brain and this leads to highly aggressive behaviors and ultimately death. There are many, many strains of the rabies virus, even if most of them are cooked up in the lab. The manipulation of this type of strain is fairly easy, making it an even more appealing method. Decreasing the likelihood of death or at least prolonging the death of the infected could be arranged with the correct strain.

Rabies behavior seems to be universal from animal to human infection. Humans experience headaches, muscle aches, vomiting, sore throat, and depression at the start. It's pretty standard cold symptoms and wouldn't draw much attention in the beginning. The latter symptoms are where the behavior gets far more interesting. This includes increased jaw pain, leading to the increased biting. Aggression and hallucinations follow. This is where the true zombie state begins.

This type of zombie behavior is fairly reminiscent of some of the behaviors you see in 28 Days Later, a cult classic if you're a zombie lover. Jerking movements, high levels of aggression, foaming mouths, lack of appetite, and low intelligence, are some of the more prominent behaviors. The behavior you won't see, the blood vomiting. That is more reminiscent of something like Ebola.

One highly interesting avenue comes from a technology that has been in development publically since the 1980s. Nanotechnology is where medical research is pressing. You may or may not have heard of it beforehand. Tiny, less than 100 nanometers, biologically engineered entities whose molecular biology can be manipulated and programmed.

This is the most terrifying set of possible behavior sets because they are fairly infinite. With the ability to spread like influenza, the hardiness of the Crimean-Congo hemorrhagic fever (CCHF), and the most aggressive traits of rabies strains could produce a super bacteria or virus that could take traits from them all. In addition, add the biologically immortal traits of creatures like lobsters or sharks to the commandeered stem cells and you have a true Walking Dead scenario.

This type of zombie would never rot because it wouldn't really be dead and would essentially be immortal until some outside force killed them. Terrifying? Yes. You would essentially create an army of truly unstoppable monsters who would attack anything that moved and who would never die.

That is probably the most significant behavior but there are the more zombie-like traits as well. Aggression would be the foremost. Like rabies, they would attack things that moved. With nanotechnology, you could specialize this. Toxoplasma gondii is a protozoa that invades the bodies of mice and programs them to be attracted to cats in order to infect the cats. If we took that trait and applied it to zombies, we could make them attracted to other humans. So far we've got aggression, targeted attraction, and biological immortality. Now add insatiable hunger to amp up the other traits.

Fast moving, aggressive, and targeted, these types of zombies would definitely be the ones to watch out for and the ones anticipate in the coming zombie war.

Nanotechnology isn't the only way to achieve this. There are selective breeding techniques that could be applied and manipulated but the nanotechnology angle seems the most likely given the current state of technology. Then again, who knows? The government has all sorts of hidden technological leaps for them to work with.

Time for Preparation

The ultimate weapon: the ability to infect thousands with a minimal incubation period, a ready-to-use army capable of massive amounts of destruction, and the ability to wage war in an incognito fashion. These are just some of the pluses to using a zombie-like pathogen to defeat a foreign army. It's hard to find a downside to using this type of weaponry. Military value for zombie agents is almost infinite. The world wouldn't know what hit it and the armies of the world wouldn't know exactly how to deal with such a threat.

That doesn't mean individuals can't prepare themselves for this military eventuality. Here are a few tips to help you get started. From there, it's up to you and ultimately a matter of good planning and luck.

Start preparation now. Delaying your prep will only put you that much more behind. There are a plethora of survival courses, prepping books, and a whole host of anti-infection merchandise that you could purchase. You can start as large scale or small scale as you want but educating yourself for off-the-grid living is key.

Get ready to cut your ties. There is safety in numbers but you're going to have finite supplies. This means you have to already anticipate your core group. Make a list proportional to the amount of supplies you can accumulate and then be prepared to enforce this list. That means your brother Joe cannot bring his girlfriend if she doesn't make the list. You have to be ready to tell Joe he can't bring his girl and be prepared for him to walk if he doesn't get his way. Harsh? Absolutely. But extra mouths to feed are extremely expensive to your resources.

Stay away from people. This one might be obvious but it needs to be said. People are going to carry infection so the more you expose yourself, the higher your risk of infection. Minimizing exposure could mean a couple of things, it might require you to evacuate the location you're in or simply isolate yourself and reinforce your current location.

Have a plan. Again, this might seem obvious but it needs to be said. When the first inklings of infection become obvious, you need to be prepared to enact a plan. First, you need to decide if you're going somewhere. If you are, prepare a backpack that will give you enough food, water, and emergency supplies to reach your final destination. Sometimes you'll hear about these bags being "bug out bags" or "Get-Away bags." They are designed to act as a ready way to escape a situation without having to spend time gathering supplies. Pack yours and place it in an easily accessible area of your closet, bedroom, or car so that when you are ready to leave, you can simply "bug out."

Speaking of vehicles, you need to make sure that you have enough gas for an entire tank for your car stored somewhere on the premises. Gas does have a shelf-life so you will have to use and then replenish your supplies every six months or so but it will be worth it when you leave and you won't have to stop for gas along the way.

Pick a Destination. If you need to escape, you need to know where you're going. You need to select your destination based on key crucial factors:

Land viability. As the lines of modernity break down, you're going to have to learn to deal with your own food. Having land that is good for growing food, hunting, and a fresh water supply is crucial to your ability to stay there for any length of time. It also might be a good idea to pick up a local farmer's almanac for the region. That way you'll be aware of particular growing seasons moving forward.

Defend-ability. The ultimate army is going to be everywhere, so you're going to have to take a good defensive position. 360-degree views and the ability to seamlessly blend into the surrounding environment.

Comfort. You're going to be shacked up for a while. A tiny house is the optimal setting and can be built relatively inexpensively with all the comforts of home. It also provides a very defensible and moveable home base since it can be built on wheels. Definitely, something you might want to consider. If you already own a stick built structure or desire to build a more permanent structure, go for it. Just realize that you may be leaving it behind.

Food is another very important factor when considering a base. Stockpiling nonperishable goods is an excellent way to give yourself some leeway when preparing other methods of getting food sources. A good rule of thumb is to have enough for three meals a day per person for at least a year.

Survival training is definitely something you should look into. With the ease of accessibility of information, you don't even have to pay for a course anymore. You can watch YouTube videos, go to survival seminars at sporting goods stores, and read online blogs. There is a lot of misinformation out there, so double check your information before relying on it.

Weaponry training. You're going to need to know how to shoot a gun, even if you never have to turn it on the undead, when society breaks down, you will have to defend yourself from those who want to take your supplies and a plethora of other problems of a post-apocalyptic landscape.

Hand-to-hand training. You may not become Bruce Lee overnight but you need to have a basic understanding of self-defense. There will come a time when bullets might not be available. There might be a time when you find yourself with nothing but a stick to defend yourself with. Knowing how to use this effectively is the only way to ensure that you will be prepared for every eventuality.

Know your sources of infection. We've already talked a little bit about how the infection could come from more sources than just a bite. Initial infection methods could come from everywhere.

Water filtration, bottled water, and similar methods may prevent exposure to waterborne pathogens. Survival filtration equipment can be expensive but the easiest method is to boil the water before using it in food or drinking water. You are not going to want to deal with any water source that has not been vetted, especially if you're not sure of the origination of the infection.

Airborne pathogens are more difficult to deal with but you can purchase protective masks to ward off any potential airborne agent. Just make sure that you are purchasing a filtered mask that has at least N95 filtration rating. This is the lowest rated filter that you will be able to use to prevent exposure. A full gas mask is preferred but simple face masks with this rating will enable you to deal with anything floating through the air.

According to the CDC, decontamination after outside exposure is necessary for you to remain infection pathogen free. While we don't have a zombie protocol as of yet, we'll give you an example of how to minimize exposure based on the Center of Disease Control's methods for preventing infection spread in a residential setting.

The entryway to the home should be cornered off with some sort of plastic material, painter's tarps and other durable plastics work well for this purpose. In this first clean room, remove outer clothing. Nothing that has been worn outside can leave this space. This will be your personal protective equipment, a facemask, outer layer of clothing, shoes, and tools. You'll leave this equipment there. If you need to wash any of the items, you'll need to use hospital grade disinfectant. You will still leave the washed equipment there for future use.

There should be a second room just past the entryway that can be created via another tarp set where you will disinfect and wash. Using hot water, you will scrub all exposed skin and hair with antimicrobial soap for at least fifteen minutes. Drying yourself requires a disposable method since you will not be able to reuse towels once they are contaminated. If you have stacks of newspapers lying around, they are a fairly absorbent material and can make decent makeshift towel during the zombie plague. Simply dispose of the newspapers in a trash bag and carry it out the next time you leave the dwelling.

After you complete this step, you are free to enter the home.

You might be asking yourself what you should do if there is a breach of infection control in your home. If a zombie busted into your house, you're going to want to clean thoroughly. Throw out all exposed porous materials like pillows, blankets, etc. All hard materials should be cleaned with gloves with hospital grade antimicrobial disinfectants. All cleaning materials need to be disposed of after use. You'll also need to reform your clean rooms again at this point and reestablish your methods for cleaning.

This might seem like hard work but if the possibility of airborne infection is imminent, it's better safe than sorry. If you are in a rural area, these sorts of infections are less likely due to the fact that the pathogens most likely will not reach rural areas, but if you are holding up in the suburbs, this is a reality that is simply too important to put aside.

When confronting the infected, make sure you cover obvious areas where infection might be prevalent are covered. Since the human bite force ranges between 101 and 174 pounds, you need a substance that is able to protect in that range. Kevlar is a great material and can be bought in handy, hand-washable shirts. Your legs are going to be difficult to cover but even taping plastic to the exposed skin will prevent bites from reaching the skin.

This protective equipment doesn't have to be bought. Most of the world's greatest ingenuities have been discovered thanks to the hard work and dedication of amateurs. The most important part of this protection is to think ahead. Think about how much protection you'll need from your head to your feet and cover accordingly.

If you expect that someone in your group may have been exposed to infection, you will have to quarantine them. This needs to be a small space where the possible infected need to be kept and observed until you are sure they are not infected. The initial observation period should minimally be two weeks, the normal incubation period for most viral exposures, but if you have more information about the bio-agent you may need to shorten or lengthen that time as needed.

If the person is cleared of infection, they should move from the quarantine room directly to the clean rooms before they can be allowed in the rest of the space.

Again, this might seem like overkill at the moment but you'll be glad that you thought of all these details when the end of the world is neigh. The better prepared you are, the better your chances are of surviving another day.

Apocalypse Now

The elite army is definitely a possibility that grows more and more plausible as time goes on. Governments are definitely constructing this new type of bio-weaponry and, unfortunately, a large swath of the population may go the way of the dinosaurs if they don't wise up.

You've taken the first step in your survival by selecting this book. A little education goes a long way toward protecting yourself and

every edge helps in a time of lawlessness and uncertainty.
We hope you find some useful information within the pages of this book and pass on this vital information to those you want to save. You never know what information will save someone's life.

Ultimate Armies through the Ages

Now we're going to have some fun with the end of the world. Here is an interesting list of the world's most elite armies that would be ravaged in a zombie attack from past and present.

The Spartan Army

Spartans are probably the historical armies which most people are familiar with thanks to the cult classic movie 300. While there were some definite exaggerations to the Spartans, like everyone having a six pack, they were quite the collection of badass warriors. The Spartan army was trained in a completely militaristic society from an early age. Raised in an almost commune fashion, they were

expected to hold bravery above all other traits.
At the height of Spartan military power, around the sixth and fourth centuries BC, it was commonly accepted knowledge that a single Spartan warrior was worth at least two of any other warriors found throughout the world. Surrender was rare and unheard of, so any hint of this sort of behavior was almost unheard of. Zombie Spartans would be terrifying.

The Roman Army

When most people refer to the Roman Army, they are referring to the armed forces deployed by the Romans and later the Roman Empire. Ancient Romans spanned a fairly long period thanks to their military prestige, lasting from roughly 500 BC to 1453 AD. These several centuries of military prestige enabled the Roman Army to make it on one of the top places in our list of top armies.
The sheer adaptability of the Roman armies during this period is one of the reasons that the Roman army was really such an overpowering military force. They went through numerous reorganizations,

equipment and tactic changes, and tactic reorganization, all while maintaining a core of military values.

For the sake of shortening the description, we'll look at the primary and longest used military organizational method for the Roman army. Based on a combination of Greek influence and Roman constructs, the army was based on an annual levy. Lower classes were the foot soldiers, the infantry ranks, and were the primary bulk of the army itself.

Calvary, the equites or celeres, aka the horse-manned solider and those who drove chariots, were composed mainly of the higher class of people known as patricians. Their wealth was the primary factor for this rank mainly due to the fact that the wealthy soldiers could afford horses and the chariot-like stations that went into battle.

The top of the food chain in the Roman army was the high king and then later the consul during the time of the Republic. The high king was the commander-in-chief until around 508 BC, when the Romans eliminated the office entirely. Consuls took the place of this ultimate commander. Consuls were given command over legions, a term that many people are familiar with.

Originally, there were only four legions but that expanded as the empire expanded their reach to every corner of the known world. Any man from sixteen to forty-six could be drafted.

Persian Immortals

One of the most well-known and most mythic armies known in many cases as simply “the immortals,” is the Persian army of elite soldiers that served the dual role of protecting the emperor as well as act as a standing army in case of imperial aggression. Though this army is known as the Persian immortals, the forces did include both Medes and Elamites.

These were heavy infantry soldiers with an array of weaponry ranging from spears to large swords. They consisted of exactly 10,000 men and everyone was replaceable. If a member was killed, sick, or wounded, another soldier was immediately put in his place, making it appear like they never lost any men at all.

The name really says it all. Maybe the immortals were actually just really elite undead soldiers. Zombie apocalypse: take two?

Macedonian Army

Led by Alexander the Great, this military force took over most of the known world and larger swaths of previously unconquered Asia. Before Alexander and his father got a hold of the army, the Macedonians weren't all that frightening. However, after increasing the size from 10,000 to 24,000 men and enlarging the cavalry from 600 to 3,500, they started on the right path toward elite army status. Coupled with those expansions, they developed the use of siege weaponry like towers and catapults.

These warriors were the epitome of the elite because the army formations required constant drilling to make sure everything ran smoothly. The hoplite phalanx of the ancient Greeks inspired a lot of the choices made for the Macedonian armies and coupled with their high-powered weaponry, they were unbeatable until their empire crumbled from being spread too thin.

It does make you wonder though, does catapulting zombies at your enemies constitute as bioterrorism?

The Mongol Army

Made famous by the larger than life presence of their leader Genghis Khan, the Mongol army was another military force that was one of the first and most elite armies in the history of military aggression. These warriors conquered nearly all of continental Asia, the Middle East and parts of Eastern Europe.

The key to the success of this army was twofold: their mobility and their adaptability. Organized with each leader functioning as the person of ultimate power over his unit, the army was essentially made of several smaller armies within the umbrella of one force. This highly flexible structure allowed the army to attack all at once, divide into smaller groups to conduct exercises like ambushes, or divide even further to eradicate any remaining armies. Individual responsibility was huge and each soldier not only maintained their own equipment and weapons but kept anywhere from three to five horses ready for battle at any given moment.

They trained in horsemanship, archery, military tactics, formations, and unit rotations. Coupled with an already nomadic lifestyle, this meant that the constant drills were always performed at "home" and the wives, herds, and children of the soldiers would accompany them to foreign lands. This comfort away from home is one of the reasons for the Mongol's overwhelming success.

The only thing scarier than a Mongol warrior is a zombie Mongol warrior on horseback.

Imperial British Army

One of the largest and most feared armies during imperialism, British military forces were thought to be an almost unstoppable force during the age of imperialism and the height of the British Empire. This was due mainly to their seemingly never-ending supply of soldiers and neat organization against foreign forces.

When speaking of the British Army, one has to understand that the term as we are using it encompasses all the military forces of the time period, including the best and biggest navy in the world. It was through the combined use of naval power and ground troops that Britain was able to expand to the colonies of the new world, other dominions and protectorates throughout the Americas, large swathes of Africa, parts of Asia, and even Australia.

This army consisted of several types of military organization that changed based on the size needs for the particular military outpost. A regiment was the formation of two or more battalions, which was the basic unit under a lieutenant colonel. Though regiment commanders rarely dealt in tactical manners, they were in charge of ensuring that supplies were accounted for and the army was properly equipped to deal with the stresses of the field. Constant recruitment in Britain and Ireland allowed the units to have a steady stream of soldiers, enabling them to never stop heading toward a target. Over time, the sheer bombardment would lead to victory.

This is the first modern elite on our list but it certainly isn't the only one.

US Delta Force

More elite and harder to qualify for than the Navy SEALs, Delta force is known as the best of the best when it comes to US military forces. It is used primarily for hostage rescue and counter-terrorism, but also functions as direct action and reconnaissance units for high-level targets. They perform many of the most highly complex and dangerous missions in the US military and are often referred to as "special mission units."

To say it's hard to get into Delta Force is an understatement. Before you are even selected you have to qualify with a series of grueling tests that consist of push-ups, sit-ups, a two mile run, and an inverted crawl over a 100 meter swim fully dressed. Next, you're put through land navigation courses including an 18 mile, all-night course while carrying a forty pound backpack. To make matters harder, the weight of the pack and the distance of the courses are increased over time while the time you have to complete the course is shortened with every march. By the end of the selection, you have a forty mile hike with a forty-five pound pack over rough terrain to look forward to. Oh, and you don't know how long you have to complete it. Surprise!

If that weren't grueling enough, there is a mental part of the test where candidates are put through a series of psychological tests designed to break them and ferret out any hint of weakness. You'll end up in front of a board of Delta instructors, psychologists, and the Delta commander whose sole purpose is to mentally exhaust you. At the end of this, you'll finally find out if you're selected for Delta.

That's just to get in! After that, the elite training really picks up and a walking, talking, military elite machine is the end result. Attrition rates are stupidly low, with only 12 to 14 men out of roughly 300 candidates making it through the selection process. That makes Delta force harder to get into than any Ivy League school in the world.

British SAS

The oldest "special forces" unit on our list dates back to 1941and is often referred to as the original Special Forces units. Their duties include some pretty hair-raising duties including: covert reconnaissance, counter-terrorism, direct action, and hostage rescue. Basically, when things go awry, these guys are sent in to fix it.

Like Delta Force, SAS is one of the hardest programs to qualify for in the military. They never recruit directly from the public, so even beginners have some sort of military starter training. Out of the hundreds of applications submitted, only a few are approved to even try out for the unit.

Selections are held twice a year and roughly compose of 200 candidates. Your try-outs are roughly five weeks and involve just as much brutal mental and physical training as you would expect from one of the most elite special training forces in the world. You have a PT test to start with and a timed cross-country march with increasing distances and weighted packs to build endurance, or break you, whichever comes first. Like Delta, this culminates in a forty mile hike with full equipment along with a repelling course that consists of both scaling and descending to finish it up. This last hike is largely jungle based training, so prepare to go somewhere with lots of mosquitos, sweat, and, no doubt, tears by the end of it all. By the end of the testing phase, candidates have to be able to run four miles in thirty minutes and swim two miles in ninety minutes or less.

Sayeret Matkal

Sayeret Matkal is the Israeli Special Forces unit which is responsible for one of the most effective hand-to-hand methods in modern society: Krav Maga. Krav Maga was invented specifically for the Israeli Defense Forces and encompasses a wide combination ancient defense arts including, aikido, judo, boxing and wrestling, as well as realistic fight training. What's really interesting about this technique is that it is known for its focus on real-world solutions. You know, instead of a bunch of Ninjas attacking you in an alley with katanas, they focus on what happens when someone comes at you with a knife. It's known to be extremely efficient and has some truly brutal counter-attacks that are guaranteed to fell any human. How well it would stack up against a zombie though, that's anyone's guess.

Sayeret Matkal is primarily a field intelligence-gathering unit for deep reconnaissance behind enemy lines. They are tasked with getting strategic intelligence to aid in other military maneuvers. In addition, they are tasked with counter-terrorism and hostage rescue missions outside of Israel's borders.

They are modeled after the British SAS and even took the unit's motto, "Who Dares, Wins."
This is still one of the places where candidates can be handpicked for recruitment though in recent years they've opened up recruitment to allow other qualified candidates to apply. Again, the only word to describe their training is "brutal." Sleepless nights, grueling hikes, and a final test that consists of a seventy-five mile hike with a full pack within a set number of hours. Ouch!
France's National Gendarmerie Intervention Group

GIGN or Groupe d'intervention de la Gendarmerie nationale, English: National Gendarmerie Intervention Group, is the elite law enforcement and special operations unit of the French National Gendarmerie. This specialized group is only 400 members strong at present but tackles some of the countries most pressing threats including: counter-terrorism, hostage rescue, national threat surveillance, government official protection, and organized crime targeting.
Created in 1974, this was supposed to be a small SWAT unit who dealt mainly in hostage

situations. They were too good for just that task thought. Since then, it's grown to nearly 400 members and has a whole host of duties to back up the need for the forces at large.

Zombies - the Ultimate Army

After looking at all the elite armies of the world, it's hard to imagine something even more elite and terrifying. The elitists of the world will be wetting themselves when they find out exactly what they will be facing when the governments of the world unleash the ultimate weapon.

The release of zombies could occur at any moment. As we've discussed in previous chapters, the development of the pathogen is already in production worldwide. So it's just a matter of time before we start seeing zombies as more than just as the occasional zombie outbreak in some Miami alleyway. Once infection spreads, the army they have created will be in full force. Let's talk about how the zombie army stacks up against its most well-trained opponents.

Specialized training is unnecessary because of the pathogen's biological programming. The need to never rest means that all the specialized training our other human armies went through is fairly meaningless. Even the most brutally trained warrior is going to need to catch some Z's.

They also don't have moral issues. Zombies aren't going to avoid populated areas or hesitate to infect small children in order to get closer to other humans. Their morale is going to flag in the least bit by emotional issues either. They're always going to be in high spirits and they're never going to lose their appetites over shocking circumstances.

Zombies don't need to be rallied before a battle. They would storm the fields with the enthusiasm of going to a theme park. It's a little like releasing a group of hungry teens in a bacon-filled all-you-can-eat buffet. The level of eagerness couldn't really be any higher.

Pain is a big deterrent for most humans. Even if the soldiers are elite, a bullet to the leg is still a massive deterrent to human beings. Zombies won't experience pain in the same manner and will not have the capacity to anticipate pain. Depending on the type of zombie behavior, rage is probably the only emotional expression available other than hunger. Snickers aren't going to cut it so

angry and hungry are probably going to go hand in hand.
The best part is that fear is also a non-factor. Even the hardiest soldiers aren't able to override all their fear factors. Zombies with their limited emotions will not experience fear as they follow the bio-agents directive to infect others and sate whatever desire that pathogen creates.
Rations are not necessary and military costs are almost nonexistent. Zombies require no lodgings, no food, and no personnel to manage them. They don't require any sort of special diet because they are able to scavenge from the enemies they take down exactly what they need.
Weaponry is also a nonfactor. After all, the zombie pathogen is a weapon in itself and any infected person will soon just add to the numbers of combatants. Furthermore, with high levels of infection, even the most careful of combatants are taking a risk every time they come into contact with the zombie hoard. Even if they are injured, zombie injuries only increase exposure risks for those injuring them.
While zombies might not experience fear, their opponents definitely do! No one faces

off against an undead horde and doesn't flinch. Even the most elite soldier is going to have some sort of hesitation and since the risk of infection is high, breaking ranks is a definite possibility.

Whatever the elite armies of the world can throw at them, zombies are going to throw it back in spades. Good luck combatting that, warriors of the world!

Chapter 10: Your Zombie Survival Kit

"I am prepared for the worst, but I hope for the best."
- Benjamin Disraeli

Now that your wardrobe is ready, it's time to prepare the rest of your person for the unthinkable.

THE BACKPACK

This is the first thing that needs consideration. You want something comfortable and spacious at the same time. On the other hand, you don't want to have too much space as that will only weigh you down.

Space

The first thing to look for in a backpack is space. Your survival kit is only as useful as the stuff inside. Weigh all your items and food and tools and see if you can find a bag that can accommodate the weight.

But you don't want a bag that can only handle as much as you want to bring. You will want some extra space in your bag. Pick one that has an expandable bottom or side to allow for more things along the way. You might pick up something important on the road like a map or a government document or more food items.

You will also want something with multiple compartments. It may sound confusing and fussy but it will actually help you categorize the items you place in your bag. Your food can go in one space, your tools can go in the other. Your maps and radios could go in another one as well.

Comfort

Of course, you'll be lugging that backpack and its contents for long periods of time. You have to be able to do so with little discomfort. Fill the pack with clothing and try it on.

See if the straps dig into your shoulders. You're looking for a bag with very wide shoulder straps because they spread the weight of the bag across your upper half, making it easier to bring. You can also look for bags with waist support/straps and sternum support for added comfort.

If you have a large enough budget to spare, you can also invest in a military-grade backpack that can be expanded and carried around easily. It is also designed to be used under conditions such as rain and hail. They can also be worn while fighting and pushing away zombies.

A Map

Be sure you don't just have a map for your city. Be sure you have a map of your whole country for that matter. You never know where the winds may take you. For all you know, everything to your right could be a zombie infested area.

As you cover more ground and discover more areas, you can mark them down on your map. You can also note your encounters and your observations. As time goes by, your map will become more and more valuable to the next person. You can end up bargaining with this treasure trove of information for food, water and ammunition.

THE RADIO

Just because you're on the road and the cell sites and servers are down, that doesn't mean you can't get information on safe zones and other important updates.

Fortunately, radio waves are sturdier than internet routers. Despite radio stations going down, you can still pick up distress broadcasts or even messages from the government through certain frequencies.

The best kind of radio you want is a hand-crank radio. This may sound old-fashioned and burdensome but it's the most economical choice in an apocalyptic situation.

You may not have the luxury of passing by an abandoned electronics store or mall to scavenge for batteries. You don't even want to wander off into those areas unless you're sure they're zombie-free. A hand-crank radio doesn't need batteries and can be used whenever you need it as long as you can operate the crank.

FIRST AID KIT

Fortunately, these come in packages when you buy them at any drugstore. They contain the most useful provisions for when you're out and about. Be sure to get something that comes in a sturdy case that is also weather-proof.

If in case you can't buy one, putting together the following items in one small bag will suffice:

A first-aid manual

Tape (adhesive for bandages)

Gauze Pads (different sizes)

Adhesive bandages

Splint

Soap
Antibacterial wipes
Alcohol wipes
Antiseptic solution
Toothache drops
Painkillers
Tweezers
Scissors
Safety Pins
Thermometer

The purpose of the kit is to enable you to administer first aid to yourself while you're out and about. You cannot always expect that you would have a doctor going around with you.

With the items above, you should be able to treat anything from wounds, bites, aches and pains that would make you less mobile in the dangerous outdoors. It would be anti-climactic if a simple toothache would be your undoing.

Since your kit will have some sharp items in it, a hard case should suffice so that they don't damage the rest of the contents.

You will also want to make sure that kit is one of the first things you can immediately see and grab from within your bag just in case of emergencies. An accessible kit can save lives.

RESPIRATOR

This may sound like movie nonsense but you can't disregard the possibility of a zombie apocalypse being caused by an airborne biochemical attack. A respirator is your best way to stay healthy in such a case.

Another reason you will want a respirator is because you'll be dealing with humans that are potentially in a decomposing state. Worse, they could be turning into something else. There might be smells that could put you off and send you reeling to your doom if you don't have a respirator.

If you do not have access to one, a simple gas mask will be a good substitute. Chances are, you'll also find yourself in bad-smelling places where there aren't a lot of people. These will help you fight the smells.

FLASHLIGHT

This goes without saying. You'll never know when you'll be sent out into the darkness from your campsite. You'll also want a flashlight just in case you get trapped inside a building without electricity.

You may not want to keep that directly inside your backpack, though. If your pack has some external pockets or slots, it should go there. It's even better if your backpack has pockets on the straps to make them accessible.

MIRROR

You may question the logic behind this at first, but a mirror is indispensable in the right hands. You can use the mirror to blind attackers at the proper angles. You can also use the mirror as a signaling device for rescue helicopters should they hover near you.

CROWBAR

Mostly used as a weapon in video games, a crowbar should be considered more as a tool. Because of its design, you can use it to pry open locked doors when you're trapped. You can also use it to open locked freezers or drawers to scavenge for supplies.

Of course, it's also good for hitting attackers in the head when you're trying to get away from zombies. Always strike using the business end of the crowbar to embed the sharp hook into their flesh to immediately dispose of them.

TISSUE ROLLS

What will seem mundane and unimportant now will be indispensable during a zombie apocalypse. Tissue paper will be one of those things. You can't just wipe blood, entrails, grease and dirt off you with your hands. You're going to need something disposable to wipe yourself with.
You also don't want to be caught in the #2 position without anything to clean yourself with. You may be on the go but you still need to urinate and defecate.

ROPE

You may need to fashion a make-shift weapon, rappel down a tall building or climb a steep rooftop. You'll need rope to do all those things. Keep several feet on your person just in case.
Besides those uses, you can also use rope to set-up traps, create detection systems and keep things together when you need to rest out in the open.

BINOCULARS

These come in especially handy when you're in unknown territory. These things will help you scout the area to find any potential threats and ways to get through blockades from a distance.

FLINT/WATERPROOF MATCHES

When night falls and you haven't found a stronghold, you still need to make camp and keep warm. Flint and a little tinder will help you start a good fire to keep your area dry and illuminated throughout the night.

Matches, on the other hand, are not as reliable as they can get wet and become useless. This is why you should go for the waterproof type so that they retain their utility no matter what the weather condition.

IRON-CAST SKILLET

Although it may seem strange to bring cookware to the outdoors, this item serves a dual purpose. Naturally, you will be able to prepare better meals over a fire with a skillet. You may not need to eat your food items raw (which is always a better alternative). With a good fire, you can also take advantage of recently-salvaged perishable items such as meat and poultry, provided that they're still good for consumption.

On top of that, the skillet also serves as a good weapon. The large circular pan of the skillet makes it easy to use. A proper swing to the head of an attacker is enough to knock them off their feet if not dispose of them on the spot.

SWISS ARMY KNIFE

They're small and come with multiple uses. From opening cans to cutting fingernails to picking your teeth, these knives are worth more than anything when you only have your wits about you. Be sure to keep one on you instead of in your backpack.

COMPASS

If you find yourself in the wilderness as you get away from urban areas, you might become disoriented and lose your way. A compass will help keep you on track while covering more ground. The last thing you want is to get stuck in a strange area with no food or shelter.

Conclusion

With the instructions in this book, you are at your most prepared for a zombie apocalypse. Despite that, there are a few things you have to remember.

First, it's not going to feel like anything you've seen on TV or in the movies. Although zombie movies and shows do a great job of stirring our imaginations, they will never feel as authentic as the real thing.

You may feel excitement and clarity when you talk about zombies now, but when an apocalypse takes place, all that confidence will be replaced with fear and confusion, regardless of how many zombie outbreak movies you've seen.

Fortunately, the only way to combat fear is with knowledge. The tips in this book will help turn you into anyone's best chances for survival. While everyone is panicking and worried about what to do, you will remain calm and collected, keeping out of trouble and slowly working towards survival.

www.ingramcontent.com/pod-product-compliance
Lightning Source LLC
Chambersburg PA
CBHW050412120526
44590CB00015B/1932
9781774856970